D0027148

"When a woman is diagnosed with breast cancer, she is thrust into a foreign world. Most, like me, look for information that will help them navigate their new reality. *Warrior in Pink* is just the book I wish I'd been able to find. Vivian Mabuni writes with transparency, warmth, and depth, and I believe all who read her special insights will be blessed and encouraged."
—Robin Lee Hatcher, author of *A Promise Kept* and *Beloved*

"Books about journeying through cancer are plentiful, but *Warrior in Pink* is different. Vivian Mabuni's honesty and faith are refreshing and uplifting. Highly recommended!"
—Colleen Coble, author of *Rosemary Cottage* and the Rock Harbor series

"Whether you are a cancer sufferer, a survivor, or someone whose world has been devastated by the cancer of another, *Warrior in Pink* will convince you that you're not alone. Vivian Mabuni tells her story in honest and helpful detail, guiding us through her learnings and revealing her discoveries of God's provision within her pain. Here's a hopeful tale for all who've spent any time in the waiting room of cancer."
—Elisa Morgan, speaker, author, and president emerita of MOPS International

"This personal look at Vivian Mabuni's journey through cancer explores how God prepares us, takes care of us, and grows us through life's difficult moments and seasons. Let this book inspire you as you journey with Vivian to discover God's love through family and the body of Christ."
—Kay Yerkovich, author of *How We Love*

"*Warrior in Pink* is a must read for anyone battling cancer, or those deeply connected to those who face that scary diagnosis. Real, raw, and chock-full of God's outrageous grace, Vivian Mabuni humanizes a difficult journey. Her story will inspire you."
—Mary DeMuth, author of *The Wall Around Your Heart*

"*Warrior in Pink* is not just a book for those whose lives have been touched by cancer; it is an inspiring story that will encourage any and all readers to stand firm in faith through whatever struggles they are experiencing. Vivian Mabuni writes with grace, vulnerability, and an observant eye that recognizes God's presence each step of the way in her battle with cancer. And as we journey together with Vivian through her story, we are reminded anew of the importance of facing our challenges in community rather than in isolation. I highly recommend this book!"

—Helen Lee, author of *The Missional Mom* and co-founder of the Best Christian Workplaces Institute

"Vivian Mabuni's story is captivating and an essential read in that every one of us will be or already has been touched by cancer. Her strength, honesty, and hope give us the tools and tenacity we need to walk through cancer (as the friend, the family, or the patient). In the midst of pain and fear Vivian brings us to hope and thanksgiving and a deeper walk with the God she loves. I highly recommend this book to anyone wondering what comes next when life hands you a diagnosis you had not planned. Vivian's words heal. Thank you, Vivian!"

—Reverend Tracey Bianchi, pastor for worship and women, Christ Church of Oak Brook, IL, and author of *Mom Connection* and *Green Mama*

"There's nothing quite like a cancer diagnosis to hurl a person into a deeper quest to understand and trust God. That happened to Vivian Mabuni. In *Warrior in Pink*, she invites us behind the scenes to enter that battle against breast cancer with her and to discover with her the power of friendship and the strength God gives His ezer-warriors, no matter what color they're wearing."

—Carolyn Custis James, author of *Half the Church: Recapturing God's Global Vision for Women*, www.whitbyforum.com

warrior in pink

*A Story of Cancer,
Community,
and the God
Who Comforts*

VIVIAN MABUNI

DISCOVERY HOUSE

PUBLISHERS

Warrior in Pink: A Story of Cancer, Community, and the God Who Comforts

Discovery House is affiliated with RBC Ministries,
Grand Rapids, Michigan.

Requests for permission to quote from this book should be directed to: Permissions Department, Discovery House Publishers, P.O. Box 3566, Grand Rapids, MI 49501, or contact us by e-mail at permissionsdept@dhp.org

The author and publisher are not engaged in rendering medical or psychological services, and this book is not intended as a guide to diagnose or treat medical or psychological problems. If the reader requires assistance, please seek the services of a physician or certified counselor.

Interior design by Michelle Espinoza

Library of Congress Cataloging-in-Publication Data
Mabuni, Vivian.
Warrior in pink : a story of cancer, community, and the God who comforts / Vivian Mabuni.
    p. cm.
  ISBN 978-1-57293-842-7
1. Breast—Cancer—Patients—Religious life. 2. Mabuni, Vivian.
3. Breast—Cancer—Patients—California—Biography. I. Title.
  BV4910.33.M33 2014
  248.8'61969940092—dc23   2013050362

Printed in the United States of America

First printing in 2014

For
Darrin,
Jonathan, Michael, and Julia.
With love.

You are undeserved blessings and evidence of God's grace.
You make any battle worth fighting.

contents

Introduction 9

1. We, Us (x 5) 11
2. Sunbeams and Southern Accents 23
3. Don't Eat Peas from Our Freezer 43
4. The Fight Is On 63
5. The Wall 73
6. The Chemo Life 81
7. Behind the Clouds 91
8. The Little Things 107
9. Room for Another 119
10. The Great Celebration 129
11. The Sensation from Swinging 137
12. Nothing Can Hurry Time 147
13. The Beginning of the End and New Beginnings 161

Appendix 1: Sherpa: Thoughts for Caretakers 169

Appendix 2: A Thousand Stitches: 173
Thoughts for Parents with Kids Still at Home

Appendix 3: Letter to a Newly Diagnosed 177
Cancer Patient

Acknowledgments 181

introduction

The LORD is the one who goes ahead of you; He will be with you.
He will not fail you or forsake you. Do not fear or be dismayed.

Deuteronomy 31:8

She had it all—described as an "Asian Martha Stewart." Her home, the food she cooked, the clothes she wore, the clothes her children wore—all flawless. But then doctors diagnosed her with breast cancer. My friend tried to reach out to her, others around her tried to help, but she refused them and shut down emotionally.

On Wednesday morning six of us met in the food court at the Irvine Spectrum mall halfway between our homes. Located between Los Angeles and San Diego, Irvine, California, boasted being the safest city in the nation. Our wicker chairs circled around a large, round metal table surrounded by potted flowers and towering palm trees. The setting described well the nature of our group and our self-appointed name: The Oasis. Week after week we unpacked our bags and filled the table with notebooks, four-color clicky pens, Bibles, coffee, and water bottles. And week after week trust grew steadily like the palm trees around us. We began to unpack the deeper places in our souls as we shared our struggles and secrets. Our choice to take time from our busy weeks to invest in building our relationship with God and each other yielded the blessing of a true oasis. Our group became a refuge and a place to refuel. Conversation came easily and we welcomed questions about the Bible. We laughed often, sometimes shed tears, and inevitably would go off on rabbit trails that eventually took us back to what we had learned in the Bible. What most groups covered in one week, we spilled over to a month.

This particular Wednesday morning Elaine shared about the Asian Martha Stewart. I leaned in to hear more. Her voice grew quiet as she struggled to share the last part.

"She couldn't handle how her body changed. She couldn't hold her perfect world together. She ended up committing suicide and left behind her husband and two kids."

The story gripped me. I had never met the Asian Martha Stewart but could relate to her desire of wanting everything together, of being the strong one, of going inside when challenged with emotional pain, of not wanting to be a burden to others. I could see myself closing off from people as she did.

The conversation probably continued around me. But in that moment I sat still. I heard the background voices and sounds of the food court, the trays and ice machines, chairs being pushed into tables, paper wrappers being crumpled. Right then, I chose to pray. "God, if anything like that ever happens to me, I purpose right here, right now, I will let others in."

I prayed this in October, two months before my life careened from the doctor call no one wants:

"You have cancer."

And looking back,

that story,

that prayer,

that moment,

that decision.

It made all the difference.

we, us (x 5)

*Therefore, since **WE** have so great a cloud of witnesses surrounding **US**, let **US** also lay aside every encumbrance and the sin which so easily entangles **US**, and let **US** run with endurance the race that is set before **US**, fixing our eyes on Jesus, the author and perfecter of faith.*

Hebrews 12:1–2 (emphasis mine)

Don't forget sugar cookies! I'd scribbled with a big Sharpie pen on one of several Post-its stuck inside my planner—one of many things to remember on this especially busy day. We finally arrived at the last Friday of school after an abnormally full week, which included a holiday orchestra concert at the high school and a Christmas dinner with the leadership board of our church. I had been up until one a.m. the night before addressing Christmas cards. The week would culminate with two class parties at the elementary school.

My six-year-old daughter, Julia, had food allergies to dairy, eggs, and peanuts. So, as with every school party and birthday party, I baked something special she could enjoy. In this case I made allergen-free, extra large sugar cookies for her to decorate in class and eat. I placed the cookies in a plastic container on the counter by the phone so I wouldn't forget.

A quick stop to get a mammogram, and then off to school to volunteer in Julia's first-grade class. Next I would pop in to eleven-year-old Michael's sixth-grade classroom to help a bit with his party and catch up with the other moms. Back into the car to head over to the high school to pick up my fifteen-year-old, Jonathan. He had early dismissal. Return to the car, drive to the elementary school to scoop up the kids, and *then* the mom taxi service would be able to park for a spell.

I looked forward to the weeks ahead as a time to exhale and take in the wonderful stretch of Christmas break. Life had multiplied in complexity. From the time school began, the kids participated in an unending, overlapping string of activities: birthday parties, marching band, soccer, football, research projects, playdates, concerts, and youth group. Two new roles for me as a graduate student starting on my master's degree along with responsibilities on a national ministry team added to the scrawl on our already full family calendar that hung by the garage door.

My husband, Darrin, and I worked for a Christian nonprofit organization, Cru (formerly Campus Crusade for Christ). After working in the Pacific Southwest Region as a regional director to the campus ministries in California, Arizona, and Hawaii, Darrin switched roles to work with the Epic Movement, the Asian-American college ministry of Cru.

I stayed home with the kids when they were young. And while I loved witnessing every first tooth, first step, and first word, my heart never stopped loving college ministry. Now with all three kids in school all day, I began to plot how I would fill the blocks of available time. Like cracking open a new journal, the blank pages brimming with endless possibilities, I anticipated the new challenges with open arms. I dove headfirst into a role serving on the Epic National Executive Team as the national director of recruiting. I welcomed the chance to engage my mind and heart in an increased capacity and work on a team with Darrin.

Along with the new ministry role, I also embarked on graduate school. It would be a slow process, taking a few classes over the course of several years, but I knew what I wanted to study and why. After years of encouraging Darrin to take seminary classes, I realized my enthusiasm originated from my own desire to enroll. So I applied and was accepted. Life moved along in high gear, but I felt centered for the first time.

Darrin's new role on the same national executive team had him visiting campuses across the country. His demanding travel schedule kept his suitcase downstairs in our bedroom rather than stored away upstairs. Running in circles at breakneck speed, our family looked forward to a couple weeks off to catch our breath and enjoy Christmas and New Year's quietly at home.

Two weeks earlier I had mentioned a suspicious lump to my new doctor. She checked and said it didn't worry her. But just in case, she gave me a form for a diagnostic mammogram. I stuffed my Bible and journal in my bag on my way out the door. As a mom of three, I squeezed in whatever scraps of time opened up to connect with God.

The mammogram took longer than I had remembered from the previous two. As we finished, the technician cleared her throat, looked at me, and then glanced away. "We need to check something out. You're going to need an ultrasound." I frowned thinking about trying to schedule another appointment so close to the holidays and expected her to say, "We'll schedule you for next week," but instead she led me out of the room. We would have the ultrasound right then. My stomach clenched, and I could feel my heart rate rising. I awkwardly grabbed my bag and held closed the ugly front-opening smock as I followed her out of the room.

We snaked around the hallway back to the same sitting area where I initially waited after I changed out of my clothes. My blueberry scone, still wrapped in the napkin from the coffee shop, suddenly lacked appeal. I nervously wiped clammy palms over my jeans. I was breathing in short, shallow breaths. In an attempt to calm the pounding in my ears, I took a deep breath and exhaled slowly. I fumbled around in my bag and pulled out my journal and Bible and tried to get comfortable on the stiff waiting room chair. All the while my hand kept tightening as I bunched the fabric to keep the smock from opening. Elevator Christmas music played overhead. With one hand I flipped to where I'd left off in my Bible reading plan. I'd been camped out in the book of Psalms, found in the middle of the Bible. Today's reading? Psalm 66. It was already colorfully underlined, a sign that those verses had significance to me in the past. This time as I read, my eyes stopped as I glanced at verse 12:

"We went through fire and through water, yet You brought us out into a place of abundance."

God impressed on my heart that He meant this verse for me—as if He laid out for me what loomed ahead—a testing through fire and water. And a promise that He would bring us out of the testing to a new place. A place of abundance.

I scribbled down thoughts and prayers in my journal until a technician called me into a darkened room. I lay down on the cold table as the ultrasound tech took measurements. The clack of tapping keys on the computer and clicking measurements sounded similar to when my pregnant belly held babies. The cold, clear lubricant smelled the same.

The technician left and returned with the doctor. I shook from the cold. The doctor, a no-nonsense woman who, judging from her direct bedside manner, I guessed had lived her formative years on the East Coast, took over. She measured and checked. She rechecked and muttered. "I don't like what I'm seeing here. No. This is not what I wanted to see."

I swallowed hard and craned my neck to try to see the computer screen. The shapes and colors on the screen made no sense.

"Is it bad?"

She looked directly at me. "I'm not going to pussyfoot around. I don't like what I see, so we are going to have to take tissue samples. After the biopsy comes back we will know for sure."

The ultrasound tech handed me a clipboard with information about getting a core biopsy. I had to read and sign papers, but could barely hold the pen steady in my hand. The technician and the doctor left to gather instruments for the procedure, and I was alone again, lying in the dark room. My shaking intensified. When they returned I focused on a spot on the ceiling and used Lamaze breathing to calm myself down. The doctor, in her straightforward approach, warned me the sound from the instrument would be loud. Clearly she had performed this procedure multiple times to know patients would find it startling. She demonstrated a practice tissue extraction in the air. The snap caused my whole body to flinch, reminding me of an amplified plastic dart gun. Similar to the shows I'd seen on the Discovery Channel when core samples were extracted from the earth's crust through a thin tube-like device, the core biopsy would take thin samples of the tissue in question. Three or four times the loud sound of the device echoed in the room. Each time my hands clenched tighter as I blinked back tears. And despite having a shot to numb the area, the procedure hurt.

After the core biopsy a nurse took me to another room to get bandaged up. She gently wrapped gauze around and around me. She gave me papers to read and sign. When she finished, she looked at me. "I am so sorry." She hugged me before she left. I found the hug odd, but comforting. I didn't remember having a nurse hug me before. It communicated to me what couldn't be said until the biopsy results came back.

When I finally left the office, I took out my phone to call my husband. Three hours had passed. My knees felt so weak and my legs gave way. I stopped and knelt on the sidewalk outside the office, making myself small. I felt somehow violated. The second I heard Darrin's voice, I allowed myself to enter the emotional weight of the moment. Tears came as the shock wore off.

"Darrin? I don't know what just happened."

"What do you mean?"

"The doctor says it's bad. After the mammogram they did an ultrasound and then took tissue samples." I didn't dare say the word *cancer* because if I did, I would not be able to recover. Instead I shifted to mama bear mode, remembering the cookies.

"Can you please take the cookies to Julia's party? Can you apologize for me for not coming? Can you go pick up Jonathan? Can you come home and be with me?"

He could tell I was shaking and scared.

I managed to make my way to the car through blurry, tear-filled vision. Inside the car I tried to calm down and look out the window as cars passed by. Everyone going somewhere. And I sat and watched.

My life—a sudden standstill.

The Awesome Threesome

When I finally made it home, I headed straight to our bedroom. I lay on the bed, pulled the covers over me, and closed my eyes. I tried to rest, but my mind couldn't settle. My prayer in the food court about letting people in came to mind. I found myself at the same crossroads of deciding whether to muster up self-sufficient strength and go all Christian Rambo—just me and Jesus—or take the braver route to open my heart and let people into my fear. My Asian heritage and cultural value of "don't rock the boat" or "the nail that sticks out gets hammered down" amplified my struggle of not wanting to bother people with my problems. I saw this dynamic played out over and over with my family and my Asian friends. One friend tweaked her back so badly she could barely walk. We had planned to have people over for a luncheon. I suggested we order out for pizza so she could rest.

"Oh no, it's okay. I'll be fine."

"No, seriously, we can cancel the whole thing or have someone bring the food. You can barely move!"

But instead of letting others help, I watched her push through the pain, and she hosted a small army in her house with a smile on her face. It was dishonorable and shameful to put people out or bring attention to themselves. I imagined the Asian Martha Stewart had similar thoughts. She ended up deciding against burdening others with her emotional struggles. I did not want my story to end like hers.

Transparency is the willingness to share about difficulties one has undergone *after* the fact. *Vulnerability* is sharing difficulties raw, in real-time, without the lesson-learned end of the story. I was comfortable with transparency. Mostly.

Vulnerability? Not so much.

I pulled out my laptop to compose an e-mail. The bandages from the core biopsy made it difficult to breathe deeply, but I also wondered if the fear of the unknown or worry about my friends' possible rejection caused me to breathe shallowly. I kept shifting around in my bed trying to get comfortable.

On the "To:" line I typed names of a handful of my girlfriends, based on who I would ask to be my bridesmaids if I married Darrin all over again. Each held a place in my heart. I'd been friends with most of these women for over two decades. I shared in the e-mail about how they made the bridesmaid selection. Cynci lived several states away; Lisa lived an hour's drive away. Three friends lived within ten minutes of me.

> Hi friends,
>
> If I were to marry Darrin again, you'd be the bridesmaids I'd pick (Cync, you for a second time). I've got not good news to share with you and am needing your prayers for this weekend and into early next week. Found a lump in my breast around Thanksgiving and went in for my annual physical. The doctor signed me up for the step up from the routine mammogram. Long story short, went to my appointment

this morning and in three hours I went from mammogram to ultrasound to core biopsy back to another mammogram for two lumps, one four centimeters, one almost one centimeter. The doctor said several times in several ways, "I am worried about this, I am very concerned about this, this does not look good, this is not what I wanted to see." More or less she wanted to let me know that it looks cancerous. The biopsy will confirm and I'll get the results back on Tuesday. I've spent time crying some off and on, letting Darrin be there for me and be strong for me. My emotions have gone from shock to fear, from grief to numbness. The waiting is the hard part right now. We are not letting too many people know until we know more details, but I did want to have some friends support us and pray for us during this initial time of shock and mixed emotions. So, please pray as the Spirit leads. Thanks.

Love you,

viv

Kelly—my friend from the University of Colorado, Boulder. "Dumb blonde jokes" in no way applied to Kelly even though she sometimes referred to herself that way. Her keen mind and learner heart gave her deep insight into Asian culture allowing her to flow effortlessly between eastern and western worlds. Her Japanese American husband, Dave, would joke that she was more Asian than he was. Kelly and I loved to sit on the couch and plan. She would take out her pencil and checkbook-size calendar and record important dates. We laughed and sighed in mutual understanding of how our husbands were drained by the very thing we so enjoyed. Faithful, loyal, generous, smart, kind, patient, humble, steadfast, and gracious, Kelly was a gifted teacher, a financial wizard, and a woman with off-the-charts integrity. We were fellow scrapbookers and annual Thanksgiving party hostesses. Over the years we took enough notes to fill a large manila folder with recipes, timelines, and seating charts until finally we could plan a feast for thirty with our eyes closed. Our kids had grown up together like cousins.

Leila—we first met before either of us married. Wise, generous, fun, passionate, thoughtful, kind, courageous, loyal, creative (an expert in color, beauty, textures, hair, interior decorating, makeup, and fashion), and an amazing question asker. Leila and I were fellow Talbot Seminary-someday-master's-degree recipients (though she is *much* further along). When her sons were five and six years old, they both planned to marry Julia. And as with Kelly's family, our kids had grown up like cousins. When times got tough on the home front we would head out, just the two of us, to Disneyland for what we called scream therapy. We would alternate between screaming on the roller coaster rides to laughing until we couldn't breathe. Time spent together playing and having fun helped restore hope and perspective, which kept us engaged in the challenges at home.

Debbie—her reputation as a godly woman, mom, wife, and leader preceded her arrival from Colorado to California. I felt honored that she would even remember my name. But God allowed me to be counted as one of her friends. The first time I heard Debbie speak, she sat in a chair surrounded by Cru staff moms from the Pacific Southwest region. I was drawn to her warmth and her bravery as she shared about the death of her infant son, Joey. Debbie came out of the darkest days of grief with her faith still intact. She spoke honestly about the hardships and challenges, but what stood out to me was her description of her church family and the blessing they were throughout their painful good-bye. I treasured time with Debbie, learning, processing, and sharing. Honest, discerning, loyal, generous, wise, thoughtful, calm, sincere, refined, intelligent; connection maker, grief counselor, conflict resolver, and gifted leader-teacher-listener, Debbie and I were fellow half-marathon-walker medal recipients. (I don't think either of us is going to do anything like that again soon. Or ever.) From the first time we met, Debbie brought calm, order, and a plan to the madness through her confidence, experience, and graciousness.

I knew I needed time to process and talk "in human" (a phrase Julia used when she was a preschooler in place of "in person"). So following the e-mail I texted these local women to see if they would be willing to meet me the next day at my Starbucks—the one with the fireplace, just around the corner from our house.

They all said yes.

The next afternoon the four of us huddled around a small wooden table meant for two. The coffee shop, always bustling and often with lines of people out the door, seemed particularly packed. But once we found and settled into our spot everyone around us faded into the background. For a few moments I stared at our Christmas-themed Starbucks paper cups on the table, and turned my cup a full 360 degrees to look more closely at the decorations for the new theme. Finally, I took a deep breath and looked each friend in the eyes.

"Thanks for being here. You guys have known me a long, long time, so you know this is a big growth step to ask you to be with me. You know what a struggle it is for me to ask for help and open up and let people in. Part of me feels kind of foolish because I don't even know the test results. Maybe meeting is all for nothing. But I realize I need your support while I wait for the biopsy results."

Kelly's eyes filled with tears. I looked at her in the silence as my eyes began to fill. Leila reached out over the table and placed her hand on my arm. I continued, my voice choking, "We've been through a lot together. Over time I've trusted each of you with the deepest parts of me. I've shared secrets and stories with you no one else knows. And I know you've done the same with me. You're not just friends, you are like family to me."

I trusted Debbie, Kelly and Leila. I knew they wouldn't try to talk me out of how I felt or carelessly quote Bible verses or try to hyper-spiritualize the situation. They knew how to sit with me in my raw emotions.

No fixing.

No advice giving.

Just listening. And being present with me in my fear and confusion.

They each showed such spiritual maturity and depth of character. Their own journeys through personal heartache helped them understand experientially what it meant to be a good friend. They were *safe*. I trusted them and they trusted me. They wouldn't judge me if I questioned God or cussed in anger or cried about possibly losing my hair.

As I shared about the events from the previous day, they held my hands. Their eyes filled with tears of empathy as they listened.

Debbie asked, after our cups emptied and my words emptied, "I'd sure like to have us pray together. Would you be willing to come over to my house?"

After feeling heard, understood, and validated, I was ready. We went back to Debbie's house to pray, welcoming the privacy her house provided. Her home became a haven. Leila, Kelly, and Debbie surrounded me as I sat on the couch. They placed their hands on my shoulders. I wept as they prayed over me.

"God, grant Darrin and Viv your peace. Peace that surpasses all understanding."

"Help them to keep turning to you. Even when they don't understand."

"Strengthen them for what lies ahead."

"Help us know how to help."

The comfort of their physical presence brought a temporary calm to my anxious heart. I didn't know the biopsy result, but I was strengthened and uplifted by these three I'd brought in to share my fears and to pray as I waited.

They became, from that day forward, the Awesome Threesome, or A3, or any number of combinations of *Awesome* and *Three* and *Wonderful*.

I'd known that life was meant to be lived in community and not in isolation. But it wasn't until I opened my life to others that I began to experience the significance of this truth. I had studied and memorized Hebrews 12:1–3, but not until I decided to let people in and feel soul-altering love through community did the repeated words of *we* and *us* stand out. I'd read the passage in the past as an individual. I focused on *my* race and the importance of fixing *my* eyes on Jesus. I still believe in the importance of each individual developing his or her own personal relationship with God, and yet, during this time, I realized how much the Bible is written with *community* in mind. The writer of Hebrews knew and stressed through repeated words the critical part people and community play in the journey of life. As I read through the first four books in the New Testament I saw Jesus' example of living life in community. He shared meals and traveled with women and men (Luke 8:1–3) and demonstrated vulnerability when He brought along His friends to be with Him in the garden of Gethsemane during the most despairing time before His death (Mark 14:33).

The meeting with the Awesome Threesome marked the beginning of my experience with true, messy community—unlike anything I had ever known before.

It marked the beginning, too, of the blessings God had for me in this journey I never wanted to take.

2
sunbeams and southern accents

So let us know, let us press on to know the LORD. His going forth is as certain as the dawn; and He will come to us like the rain, like the spring rain watering the earth.

Hosea 6:3

I waited for the call from the doctor through the weekend and into the third day—three days before Christmas. Darrin and I had a fight earlier in the day and tension still lingered in the air. The stress from this time of year made conflict predictable, and the combination of excessive activity and fatigue only intensified our emotions. My attempts to create Christmas magic like I had seen in Hallmark commercials further fueled our conflict.

In the pretend world of television and commercials, houses were spotless; kids had great attitudes; husbands and wives looked adoringly into each other's eyes; and misunderstandings could be cleared up in thirty minutes. The greater the distance between reality and expectation, the greater the disappointment. But this day I felt edgier than normal, distracted, and not very present. The stormy winter weather matched my mood as the rain, twisted together by the wind, splashed against our windows like a broken sprinkler.

My cell rang, and I looked for someplace private to take the call. I walked into the garage and closed the door to my office, which happened to be my car. Sitting inside the car, inside the garage, I found my familiar haven. With three kids and a constant stream of places to be, things to do, people to talk with, this place became my refuge, my place to regroup and sometimes even catch a nap. This time, however, I can't remember even breathing. I fumbled to open the storage compartment to grab a pen and whatever paper I could find. The doctor said in a matter-of-fact tone, "I have your biopsy results. The pathology report shows you have invasive lobular carcinoma."

I scribbled down the words, trying to sound them out. Something about pathology and those three foreign words. I cleared my throat, scribbled little circles on the corner of the paper to start the ink flowing again, and asked, "Wait. What does this mean?"

"I'm sorry. The biopsy shows you have breast cancer."

I had no words.

The doctor broke the silence. "You're going to need to come in tomorrow to talk with a nurse practitioner. She will help you navigate your next steps. I'll put you through to the appointment desk."

The appointment set, I sat stunned in the passenger seat of the car.

The familiar creak of the door. Darrin walked into the garage. He stood by the car as I got off the phone. Our eyes met as I opened the door. After seventeen years of marriage, he could read me well. My face was probably pale, my eyes dry. But he knew. Then, as if a spell that had kept us suspended in ignorance broke, the words tumbled out of my mouth.

"It's cancer. The doctor says it's cancer."

Saying the words out loud, *those* words out loud, snapped me from cognitive knowledge to the here and now of that moment. I collapsed in his arms, sobbing.

Darrin is the strongest man I know—a modern-day Jean Valjean. He carried our refrigerator on his back up a steep flight of stairs to our apartment when we lived in West Los Angeles. And there in the garage, he stood strong as an oak and held me. And while my shoulders shook and I struggled for breath, and as my tears dampened his T-shirt, he did what came most naturally to him in crisis.

He prayed.

His words were simple and honest. His voice was soft and sure. "Father, thank you that you are here. We don't know what all this means. We're scared, but we trust you. Please guide and direct our steps. We love you. In Jesus' name. Amen."

When he finished, the garage was quiet. I opened my eyes. The sky outside must have cleared briefly, as a single sunbeam came through the small glass window on our garage door and landed right where we stood in a hexagon of warm sunlight—a gift for us. As if God spoke, "I am here. I am near. I am with you as you walk through this."

After I calmed down, we went back inside, mentioned something about last-minute Christmas shopping to the kids, and hurried out of the house. Mostly, we were in shock. Our earlier fight faded into the background. We drove to Laguna Beach and stood on the pathway outside one of our favorite brunch spots that overlooked the ocean. In silence we looked out over the water. The ocean sounded angry, the dark waves crashing mercilessly onto the rocks below. Dark gray clouds threatened more rain. Then Darrin touched my arm and pointed to the horizon. In the distance we saw faint rays of sunshine break through the clouds.

I held onto those sunbeams. They spoke hope to me in the midst of this new storm.

That night, I went to bed feeling nauseous as I turned over and over in my mind the reality of cancer.

The next day we left the house informing the kids we had more last-minute shopping to do. We had decided to wait until after Christmas to tell the kids and our family. On the agenda was a meeting with a nurse practitioner to go over my test results, followed by an MRI. After the procedure we would meet with a genetic testing counselor.

As Darrin and I sat down in the small barren office, my emotions matched the surroundings—sterile and cold. Thankfully, the compassion the nurse exuded helped to warm the room. She presented two thick folders—my medical file and a file full of reading material about breast cancer. She took out a black pen and began drawing a diagram on a blank page. She explained, "Your cancer cells are moderately differentiated."

I guessed, based on the tone of her voice, that this was a good thing.

"That means you don't have the fast-growing cancer cells."

Definitely a good thing.

I looked up from the page and asked, "Can you explain what invasive lobular carcinoma means?"

"Well, invasive means it's spreading." She opened a folder to a diagram of a breast and pointed with her pen. "The most common type of breast cancer is ductal—meaning they're contained in a milk duct. Yours is lobular, which means outside of the milk duct. That means two things. First, the tumor is large and tentacle-like, and second, studies showed a higher percentage of recurrence of this type of cancer in the other breast. And carcinoma means cancer."

"Wait. What did moderately differentiated mean again?" I blink backed tears and looked down at the notes I took on one of the handouts she gave me. I could tell the nurse had explained these terms before. I stared at the folder full of pamphlets feeling frozen, unable to form words. I felt like I was in a bad dream about to take a final

I didn't study for. Darrin took my hand. The warmth from his hand steadied me temporarily.

"I know this is a lot of information to take in. My phone number is on the card so you can call me anytime with any questions that come up. Seriously. Any questions. Anytime." I felt she was on our side and was looking out for my best.

She continued, "It's important for you to gather together a medical team as you battle cancer. And this will most certainly be a battle. You will be working with several different doctors. The doctor who performs the surgery to remove your tumor, the surgical oncologist, will not be the same doctor who will treat you during chemotherapy."

"But I thought I would have the same doctor all the way through."

"No. You will undergo chemotherapy with a different doctor—the oncologist. And should you need to undergo radiation treatment, you will be seen by another doctor—a radiation oncologist."

Darrin squeezed my hand to reassure me.

"Our hospital has a group of doctors who all know each other and have worked together for years. They meet on a weekly basis to discuss each case and suggest treatment options. You will want your medical team to be on the same page as you undergo treatment."

She handed me a list of doctors who were covered by our insurance. I scanned over the names. I didn't know what some of the descriptions following their names meant. I sat there, shaking my head. "Where do I even begin? Who would you recommend I call?"

My head swam. Numb from shock at the diagnosis, I still had to make decisions about treatment options. I took in the information feeling oddly separate from my circumstances. I pushed aside the reality that I sat in an office discussing a cancer diagnosis—*my* cancer diagnosis—with my husband. I *had* to push it aside in order to not fall apart. I needed to absorb as much information as possible.

The nurse touched my arm and looked us both in the eyes.

"The one thing I want you to take away from our time is that cancer doesn't necessarily equal death."

She slid our breast cancer information packet across the desk to us. She pointed to her file. "You need to know that people these days often battle cancer multiple times in their lives. From the information gathered here, your prognosis looks good."

I left the office thinking about battling cancer. I was now a warrior in pink but I didn't feel brave or strong like I pictured a warrior. I was scared.

Darrin held the mound of reading material in his arms. I clutched my purse up against my chest, grabbing for anything that would help anchor me. I felt dizzy from the onslaught of new terms from this new world. Terms I never knew existed.

Terms I wished I still didn't know.

Christmas Aftershock

We managed to enjoy a quiet Christmas Eve and Christmas morning, but food and festivities all seemed muted as though I observed the celebrations from the outside. I kept looking at the kids.

How would they take the news?

What would the following year would hold for them?

I took pictures of them as they looked through our cranberry-colored Christmas photo album. Years earlier, overwhelmed with the sheer volume of photos that filled boxes in our storage, Kelly and I decided to participate in a Creative Memories scrapbook party. Instead of Creative Memories, we called ours Desperate Memories. Rather than catching up chronologically on every event in each child's life, I decided to put together a few albums around themes: Thanksgiving, birthdays, and Christmas. Each year I would add just a few photos and some descriptions to help record our family memories. Now I watched silently as the kids flipped through the pages. They laughed and pointed at the pictures from previous years. I gripped the camera tighter as I wondered, Would I be around the following year to add more pictures to the album?

A few gifts sat under the tree. Ones we hadn't yet sent to our family. Darrin's family lived in Hawaii; my sister lived in Colorado; and my parents resided in Nevada. As I looked at those gifts, I realized again how our immediate family lived far, far away. Our families had missed so many milestones and celebrations because of the distance, and now with the weighty news of my cancer diagnosis, the distance felt farther.

After breakfast, with bits of wrapping paper and ribbons still scattered across the wood floor, Darrin called the boys to sit with us at the dining room table while Julia lost herself in her new pile of toys. He looked across the table at me, nodded silently, and then cleared his throat.

"Boys, we don't know how exactly to say this, but mom was diagnosed with breast cancer right before Christmas."

Normally the boys fidgeted and poked at each other. With Jonathan halfway through his first year of high school and Michael in sixth grade, his final year of elementary school, the age gap of three years between the boys seemed even wider. Still, they knew which buttons to push to set each other off. Our family meetings were notoriously long due to their teasing and jabbing. Now, they sat completely still, eyes wide. Their silence caught me off guard.

Darrin continued. "We don't know what this means yet, but we will let you know what we know when we know. Right now we want you to know the nurse we met with said mom's prognosis looks good. What that means is she thinks mom will make it out of this okay. She will have surgery to remove the cancer and maybe chemotherapy and radiation."

They shifted their gaze from Darrin, sitting on one side of the table, to me as I pretended to cough to push back my tears. I asked weakly, "Do you guys have any questions?"

I could see they both were in shock. *We* were still in shock. This news came out of nowhere. Michael looked down as he traced the pattern on the Christmas tablecloth with his finger. Then he looked at me.

"Did God give you cancer?"

His question pierced me. From the time he was born my most consistent prayer for my kids was for them to embrace a relationship with God for themselves. I prayed they would own their own faith. And now I wondered how his questions would impact his understanding of a loving God.

I reached out to touch his arm. "Oh, Buddy, you are asking a good question. No. I don't think God gave me cancer, but for some reason He is allowing me to have cancer. I don't know if this makes sense, but cancer and other sickness exists because we live in a fallen world. It's not the way God intended."

Darrin added, "Just because we follow God doesn't mean hard things or bad things won't happen to us. But we will walk through this together. God will help us. Mom and I will answer any questions you have and we will let you know what we know."

Sitting there, watching my children's faces, I realized my cancer would stretch all of us. A whole set of questions would arise like the one Michael asked. We decided to tell them honestly what we knew so they wouldn't have to guess or draw conclusions from silence. We also decided we would try and keep life as normal as possible, so the kids would be able to enjoy their various activities.

Cancer may have come into our lives, but we would not let it overtake our lives.

We sat down later in the day to tell Julia. Sitting on our couch, I wrapped my arm around her shoulder.

"Sweet Pea, we need to talk with you. Have you heard of the word *cancer?*"

She nodded, frowning.

My heart ached as I touched her frown and brushed away her hair from her forehead. I didn't want to tell her. "Well, Mommy found out a few days ago that cancer is growing in her body."

Tears filled her eyes. She threw her arms around me. At the tender age of six, she still approached life unfiltered.

Darrin patted Julia on the back, stroked her long hair, and explained, "The nurse says they think Mommy will be okay. The doctors will get rid of the cancer. She will have an operation and maybe have medicine to zap away the cancer cells."

She wept despite our attempts to reassure her that the prognosis looked good. I struggled to hold back my own tears, wanting to be strong and positive for her. The puzzle pieces re-formed in her mind, and it finally made sense why I missed her Christmas party at school. That realization only added to her tears.

A few nights later as I put her to bed, Julia confided to me that she knew people died from cancer, and she worried she would lose her mommy. Like every parent, when faced with our own children going through pain, I would have done anything to keep her from walking the road ahead of us. I felt so helpless! If only we had a fairy-tale charm that could magically remove all her fears and her worries. But life doesn't always obey fairy tale endings.

If only my fears and worries would go away, too.

As each day rolled into the next, the truth of cancer settled into me. Knowing cancer's reality, my emotions traveled through every imaginable feeling. Often all in the same hour. I felt scared about the operations, about going bald from chemo. I felt sad for my kids. I felt worried about how my diagnosis would affect Darrin. I felt angry every time I remembered I had cancer. At times I felt bewildered because I felt fine physically. I'd been running three to four miles every other day. How could cancer be growing in my body? It just didn't make sense. And I didn't know how to make it make sense. For my family.

Or for myself.

They Go from Strength to Strength

Each morning I woke up in the dark, wondering if all that had happened was a bad dream. Then reality would hit anew and my mind would race into overdrive. I crawled out of bed, morning after morning, while the whole house slept, and made my way up the stairs to my nook, where I poured out my disbelief and concerns to God in my journal and read from the Bible. I read verses that seemed written just for me:

> *Blessed is the man whose strength is in You,*
> *whose heart is set on pilgrimage.*
> *As they pass through the Valley of Baca,*
> *they make it a spring;*
> *the rain also covers it with pools.*
> *They go from strength to strength;*
> *each one appears before God in Zion.*
> (Psalm 84:5–7 NKJV)

The Valley of Baca, also known as the Valley of Weeping, and the phrase "*as* they pass" reminded me that the Valley of Weeping is part of life's journey. Sooner or later, everyone passes through their own valley like this.

These verses spoke hope that good could come of my valley, making it a place of refreshing springs. Again, the picture came to me of journeying through fire and water toward a place of abundance. God could be trusted to provide rains of blessings, pools to drink. He would refresh me along the way, and I would venture from strength to strength. God would provide, as He so faithfully had done in the past, the needed strength to walk through this new trial. I would not need to muster up my own strength; instead, my strength would be *in* God and come *from* Him. This strength could not be collected or stored up, but would be enough for each day.

I loved thinking about going from strength to strength. As I looked back over twenty-seven years of dependence on God, I could say with confidence He had been faithful. I hadn't always known God in a way where I felt close enough to depend on Him. I didn't grow up in a religious home. I considered myself a spiritual person and knew a spiritual dimension existed beyond the five senses, but in my mind God was distant and too busy with other problems to bother with me. During high school I began to notice a void in my life that awards, money, relationships, and material things could not fill. During this time my friend, Jean, who sat next to me in math class, began to change before my eyes.

"Jean, what's happened to you? You're different now. You seem to glow."

Jean threw her head back and laughed, her eyes shining, "Is it that obvious? Am I *really* glowing?"

"Well, yeah, something's going on. You're not the same."

We stuffed our books into our backpacks and walked out into the crowded hallway toward our next class. Raising my eyebrow and tilting my head I gave her a look that said, "C'mon, don't keep me in the dark. Explain yourself."

"Viv, something wonderful has happened to me. I've become a Christian. I have a personal relationship with God now."

"What do you mean, personal relationship? Doesn't going to church make you a Christian? And really, *you*? A Christian? You're smart. You can't possibly believe what's written in the Bible. That thing is full of contradictions. Christians are narrow-minded hypocrites. They think they have the only religion."

The following weeks and months I continued to pepper Jean with questions and protests. But the change in her life and in her countenance was undeniable.

Sitting in my room after school, Jean explained, "Christianity is not about practicing a religion, Viv, but it's about being in relationship. Religion is man trying to reach God. Christianity is God reaching down to man through Jesus. I committed my life to Jesus. He loves me and I have chosen to follow Him. My relationship with God has been restored. All of us are separated from God because of sin. Jesus took my place and died for my sins. Now I'm forgiven. I'm free."

Oh, no! I thought. Jean had become a Jesus freak.

How could Jean, brilliant and witty, fall for this blind faith? How could she decide to follow a God who allowed so much suffering in the world? How could she be sure Jesus was really God?

But I found myself drawn in as she shared about her relationship with God. It was dynamic and intimate and unlike anything I had known. No longer distant and far away, God showed up in Jean's life in tender ways. This heightened my awareness of my own spiritual void. Jean's faith journey set me on my own faith journey. I began to ask questions about the Bible, about the problem of pain, about all the other religions. I read books and studied about the reliability of the Bible. I learned the Christian faith had a solid intellectual base. The personal dimension began when I started writing letters to God. To my surprise, He answered my queries. God brought the right people at the right time. I learned entering a relationship with God involved my intellect, emotion, and will. By the end of the school year, the summer before my junior year in high school, I, too, committed all I knew of myself to all I knew of God and entered into a love relationship with Jesus.

Though I had a new relationship with God, I found trying to live life as a Christian incredibly frustrating. I needed a Bible so I drove myself to a bookstore in the mall and bought one. Reading it made no sense. I knew Christians prayed, but I fell asleep each time I tried. I drove myself to church and cried through all the worship songs and then drove home unchanged. Now I knew right from wrong, but it seemed I continued to choose wrong.

My first lesson in God's mysterious ways and His faithfulness came the following year. My father decided to move our family, after seventeen years in Boulder, Colorado, clear across the ocean to Hong Kong right before my senior year. As you can imagine, my parents had to drag me over by my heels, my nails leaving behind scratch marks all 7,452 miles.

I had plans to participate in *everything* my senior year, but now my plans were cast aside. I dreaded moving to Hong Kong. Not only did I not know anyone my age there, everyone spoke Cantonese—and I grew up speaking Mandarin. Though the Chinese characters were the same, the pronunciation was completely different. Besides, I couldn't read more than twenty Chinese characters.

When we finally settled into our new home, I railed at God for allowing this horrible event in my life. My prayer to him went something like this:

"I am so ticked off at you! I can't believe you would let this happen to me! This is my senior year! I had plans! Why Hong Kong? I can't understand what anyone is saying on TV or on the street. I hate it here. It's hot. And humid. And my friends are far away."

I took a breath and paused. In barely a whisper I continued, "But in my heart of hearts, I really want to know you. I need a church, a youth group, some Christian friends. If you provide that, I will give you my whole life. I will hold nothing back. Otherwise, I'm going to go out and do something I'll probably regret, but I'm never talking to you again!"

Shortly after the prayer, I got involved with the debate team at Maryknoll Convent School, the all-girl's Catholic school I attended. Maryknoll, one of the top schools in Hong Kong, sat at the corner of a busy intersection in Kowloon. The beautiful architecture, intricate European design, and distinct orange bricks looked out of place compared to the stark white buildings surrounding the school. Girls who attended Maryknoll wore their school uniforms with their heads held high.

The school system in Hong Kong followed the British system. Instead of grades, students were divided into forms. After Form 5 (the equivalent of junior year in American high school), hundreds of students took extensive exams. Those with the highest scores were given one of thirty-six available spots in Form 6. Somehow I garnered one of those spots.

I had never been in a more academically challenging environment than my time at Maryknoll. They taught classes in English, but students bantered in Cantonese. When I heard the debate team debated in English, I decided to take part. The girls on my team became my closest friends there. Following one of the debates, a boy from the rival boy's school approached me.

"Excuse me. Are you a Christian? Would you like to come to our youth group?"

My jaw dropped and I looked up to the ceiling. God worked fast!

"Um. Yeah. I'd love to check out your youth group. Can I bring my sister?"

The following Friday I attended the youth group at the Christian Missionary Alliance church, which turned out was walking distance from my school and our home. The first lesson I learned that night centered on living a Spirit-filled life. How did the youth pastor know this teaching filled in what went missing in my failed attempts to live as a Christian?

I learned that night the Christian life wasn't hard to live. In our own human effort, the Christian life was *impossible* to live. But God supplied the power source. Reliance on Him and His Spirit enabled us to live as Christians. Most Christians, like me, didn't know about this power source. Either ignorance or rebellion kept too many from living a life truly surrendered to God, a life set apart by and for Him.

All the things I had clung to so tightly in high school, the things I thought gave me purpose and worth, were stripped away when we moved to Hong Kong. But the seeming loss brought about a spiritual awakening. I followed through on my half of the prayer and gave God control of my life. I would hold nothing back. I was willing to go anywhere and do anything.

And a remarkable thing happened.

I felt alive in a way I had never known before. Hong Kong started off as an undesirable change in my plans and ended up holding a place in my heart as the place where my relationship with God became intimate. I wouldn't trade the experience of finding God and living in Hong Kong for anything.

From that point on God had showed himself trustworthy in countless ways over the years as I made choices to trust Him. Now I would need to remember and recall and draw on His character as I moved ahead into a new area to trust Him: battling cancer.

Life Is Precious

A few days after Christmas, Darrin and I met with my surgical oncologist. Two qualities about her caught my attention. She had the distinct description of being the only female surgical oncologist in South Orange County, California. She also walked each day as a breast cancer survivor, a fellow warrior in pink. In contrast to the other doctors' offices I visited, her office felt welcoming. The waiting room walls, painted in warm, rich colors reflected beauty and femininity.

A comfortable couch was a welcome change from the plastic waiting room chairs in other offices, beautiful Christmas decorations had been placed with care, and classical Christmas music played overhead.

As we sank onto the couch, it hit me how life had taken a dramatic turn. Those decorations stood in stark contrast to how our life felt. I struggled to hold back tears—and failed. A nurse came out to the waiting room carrying cups of tea and coffee. Her kind, calm, deep blue eyes reflected understanding. "The Lord is with you," she said. "He is going to see you through this. I was diagnosed with breast cancer fourteen years ago around the same time, Christmastime, so I know how you may be feeling."

Darrin and I looked at each other stunned.

"I saw in your paperwork that you work for Cru. My husband and I love your ministry and what you do. We've supported staff like you through the years."

I started crying, but these were different tears. Ones of appreciation to God for allowing my path to cross at just the right time with just the right person. Here standing before me was a woman who understood firsthand the myriad emotions I felt. She would be the first of many brave warriors in pink who would share their stories, hug with understanding, and offer hope through their presence.

During the two-and-a-half-hour appointment, I learned the tumor was too large for a lumpectomy, so my treatment following surgery to remove both breasts would require chemotherapy and possibly radiation. I collected another large file of pamphlets and articles to add to my growing stack of reading material. Yet again I realized how similar this process was to pregnancy. Then as now, I read everything I could in preparation for what loomed ahead. Except this information did not enlighten about the development of new life. This information had to do with the prevention of death.

The following weeks I underwent a PET scan, CT scan, chest X-ray, and echocardiogram. I had heard terms like MRI, PET, and

CT scans before, but had never experienced any of the procedures. My seasonal, horrible head cold made it hard to breath through my stuffed nose. Instructions to lie completely still while holding back my coughs added another challenge. Any major movement and we would have to start all over. The loud sound of the MRI whirling around me reminded me of how it felt to stand next to a small propeller plane. The technician put headphones over my ears and piped music in to help pass the time. I brought in a personal CD from a student band of one of our Cru ministries on the Central Coast.

I most remembered the radioactive liquid from the PET scan. A nurse carried the vial in a padded container with a hazardous liquid symbol on the outside. I looked away at a spot on the wall as she inserted the IV into my vein. I winced in pain. Each prod and poke reminded me of how I disliked needles. Three or four different times she asked if I ever had an allergic reaction to shrimp or iodine. I was fairly certain I had not. I worried what would happen if my body reacted violently to the hazardous liquid. The nurse opened the flask, took out a tube, and slowly pumped the liquid into my body through an IV. Next I had to wait almost an hour in the dark while

CaringBridge

Breast cancer. For me these two words together stir up anguish and even mild shame. Other cancers seem easier to talk about (except maybe colon). But I am faced with battling cancer in part of my body that is both personal and private. Now I have to make decisions about my cancer treatment with a medical *team*. I also have to figure out the if, how, and when of reconstruction as part of my cancer journey.

I'm an on-the-younger-side woman and foremost on my mind is preventing cancer's return. The type of cancer I have, invasive lobular carcinoma, has a higher percentage of recurrence. If I landed in the "grandma" category, I probably would not opt for reconstruction. If I were younger and planned on having more children, I probably would choose to have a single mastectomy. But I'm past the nursing babies life-stage. So I've decided to have a double mastectomy and reconstruction at time of surgery. I based this decision on not wanting the kids or Darrin to have to walk through cancer treatment again, if possible.

This means I will have one less operation and hospital stay but a more difficult recovery and more pain while undergoing chemo. I want to spend the shortest time possible in treatment and recovery. I'm told some women postpone reconstruction until after active treatment to give their bodies and emotions ample time to heal. For me, I'd rather get everything over with at once.

Overwhelmed by the sheer number of medical appointments and treatment decisions, I impulsively chose reconstruction at time of surgery without talking through the decision with Darrin. If I could go back in time, this is the one thing I would change.

the liquid worked its way through my body, warming every inch.

The whole body scan took about twenty minutes. The technician placed me in a tube and gave instructions to not move and to breathe slowly. The PET scan would show if cancer had spread to other parts of my body.

In forty-two years, I had never had so many procedures and sat in so many waiting rooms as I did in those few weeks. I had no idea how much all of the doctors' appointments, testing, surgeries, and chemotherapy treatments would end up costing. As missionaries with Cru, we were dependent on the donations of churches and individuals to fund our ministry and pay our salary and health insurance. We had little saved in our emergency fund. Cancer treatment seemed like it would require an obscene amount of money.

Once, when I asked Darrin about the bills, he took my hand, his grip strong and sure. "We could always sell the house and live in a box. Whatever it takes."

I knew if the tables were turned and one of the kids or Darrin battled cancer, I wouldn't hesitate to do whatever we needed to preserve their lives.

Whatever it takes.

Still, the idea that all of this time and money focused on preserving my little life—one little life—humbled and overwhelmed me.

Life is precious.

And I was learning that *my* life was precious.

Worth saving.

My thoughts moved to Jesus' great love. He gave His life in order to preserve mine. His attitude reflected the ultimate "whatever it takes." He gave everything for us to be with Him. For me to be with Him.

Even dying in my place to secure my life.

I learned in new ways how valuable people are to God.

And to me.

Jesslyn

For three years I carried around a little picture from a magazine of this haircut I loved. I kept it in the little zipper pocket in my purse and transferred it to each new purse. I chickened out every time I went in for a haircut. Every. Single. Time. Jesslyn, my stylist, would smile and say with her wonderful, soothing Alabamian accent, "It would look great on you, so whenever you're ready."

Jesslyn and I met back when our now-teenagers were in preschool singing in the Little Lambs choir at Saddleback Church. At the time of my diagnosis, she'd been cutting my hair over eleven years. No other stylist had touched it since I met her. In fact, Jesslyn knew I was pregnant before I did just by washing my hair and recognizing a difference in the texture! From that point on I knew she would be my stylist for life.

But she wasn't the only one I'd showed the haircut picture to. I showed most of my friends—and even strangers—the picture over the years and *everyone* agreed it was a *really* great cut. Three years of *unzip*, "Love this haircut," return to pocket, *zip*, repeat.

Until the diagnosis.

My son Jonathan, Mr. Cool-High-Schooler with on-the-longer-side hair, asked me before I left, "Does this mean your hair will be shorter than mine and you're going to give me a hard time about my hair being longer than yours?"

I grinned at him. "Buddy, pretty soon *everyone* will have hair longer than I do." It felt good to share a laugh as I left the house.

A short time later I walked up to Jesslyn, the picture in hand. "It's time." And she did her magic.

Leila accompanied me to the hair appointment and took pictures. My emotions flew up and down. I finally felt free to be bold and take a risk to get the cut I'd always wanted, because in three months' time I would be bald with no hair *to* cut. I asked Jesslyn if she would shave my head once chemo kicked in.

She, of course, willingly agreed. But for now, I would enjoy the new haircut. As she finished up she said, "This one is on me."

I choked up over her generosity. All three of us had tears in our eyes. Her kind gesture overwhelmed me. I tried to collect myself as I left, but once we got outside Leila and I hugged and cried on the sidewalk outside the salon.

The hair thing?

A big deal.

Really.

But once again I experienced God's love and presence through His people. I would not battle alone.

I figured it would be nine weeks of super short, super sassy haircut enjoyment before going bald.

Now. Now was the time.

3
don't eat peas
from our freezer

I lift up my eyes to the hills. From where does my help come? My help comes from the LORD, who made heaven and earth.
Psalm 121:1–2 ESV

I haven't always been a runner. Actually, I'm still not a runner. Over time I evolved to a *sort of* runner. Several years back, when we hit our milestone birthdays of turning forty and fifty, Debbie convinced me to attempt something new. We would wake up in the shivering cold—well, as cold as southern California gets, which really isn't *that* cold. But it was cold and dark when I reluctantly climbed out of my warm bed to train for the Huntington Beach Half Marathon—all 13.1 miles. No way I could or would ever run that far, but Debbie seemed to think we could *walk* it. Debbie was the only one I would wake up for in the cold and dark. Time to walk and talk with her made training to walk a half marathon worthwhile.

Our first morning, Debbie arrived with a printout. She had devised a four-mile adventure through the neighborhood—which included three monster hills. The biggest one I named the "ultra-mega-steep" hill. A San Francisco–category hill that caused walkers to lean at a forty-five-degree angle and talk in short breaths. We got lost the first few times out, but after awhile the route became so familiar we could find our way home—even in the dark.

As the days blended to weeks, the sky grew lighter earlier and hills became more manageable. The rich conversations Debbie and I shared processing life, identity, motherhood, marriage, and ministry kept me from noticing the burn in my legs. One conversation began to change the way I viewed myself.

Debbie had returned from Synergy, a conference for ministry leaders in Florida, with several of our mutual friends. She shared highlights from the conference as we worked up a sweat aggressively tackling the hills.

"One highlight for sure was hearing Carolyn Custis James speak. Have you heard of her?"

I nodded. Out of breath and longing for the warmth of my bed and my feather pillow, I kept willing one foot to go in front of the other.

Debbie continued, "She brought to life the passage in the Bible from Genesis 2:18 describing Eve. *'Then the Lord God said, "It is not good for the man to be alone; I will make him a helper suitable for him."'* Eve was tasked to be Adam's helper. As a wife, I had understood the passage to mean helping my husband with what he needed, but Carolyn taught us the Hebrew word used for helper. Her explanation vastly expanded my limited view."

Debbie's words piqued my curiosity. We headed along at a quick clip on the flat portion of our walk.

"God used the word *ezer*. It rhymes with razor. It's used twenty-one times in the Old Testament, sixteen of those times as a description of God himself."

I tried repeating the word.

"Do you know what context in which the word was most used? Military battles. Women were called by God to be *ezers*—strong warriors. Together with men, *ezers* would learn to use their unique gifting and experiences to engage in fighting darkness and injustice."

Hearing this description of women inspired me profoundly. It stirred in me newfound purpose and perspective. I looked over at Debbie, "So what you're saying is an *ezer* will never be sidelined."

Debbie nodded.

I let her words sink down as hope sprung up. I spent countless hours meeting with college students and investing my life mentoring, training, and equipping them. I felt like I was on the front lines of battle before having kids. But realizing my call to be a warrior in every season opened my eyes and called me to live on purpose in my current life stage. Fighting for my marriage and my family, interacting with parents at the soccer games, opening our home to others, teaching Bible studies, sharing our lives and our resources, all of those things mattered. My role as an *ezer* warrior would be constant, but the landscape of where I would battle would look different in every season. As a warrior, God would allow both times of training and times of battle. Now, two years later, I found myself returning to this conversation as I faced my cancer battle. I was a warrior, an *ezer*. This time my call was to fight and be fierce while robed in pink.

Debbie and I continued to train. We kept showing up. When race day finally arrived, our training paid off, and we finished the race. After we received our medals for completing the half marathon walk, I swore I'd never walk again because my arms almost fell off. I anticipated my legs dying, but my arms? Who willingly walks, swinging their arms, for 13.1 miles straight? Following the race I walked around for days unable to lift my arms even to brush my teeth.

But several months after the half marathon, the pain became a distant memory. I kept walking our route, but decided one morning to set a goal to get to a place where I could run the entire Debbie's Course without stopping—hills and all. It took a *long* time, but little by little I built up strength and endurance to tackle those hills. The day I finally ran the whole course without stopping, I celebrated in my kitchen dancing with my arms overhead as the theme song from the movie *Rocky* played in my heart.

Now, with this unexpected, out-of-the-blue cancer journey, the hills on Debbie's Course represented the road ahead. The first big hill would be surgery and recovery. The next hill, chemo. And the final hill, should I have to face it . . . radiation. Little did I know how much I would need to return to this image of a warrior runner during the months of treatment and even the year following. My eyes and ears attended to stories of people *battling* cancer. It certainly was wartime.

The procedures for this unwelcome medical trial kept changing. Originally I thought I only needed to go through surgery. I could handle that—two to three months of medical treatment. Then the doctors added chemo, which increased the timeline another four months. I came to a stunning realization: cancer had permanently altered my life. Even in remission I would still be tested, tracked, and checked. The rest of my life.

No one could tackle these hills for me, though I knew many who would take my place if they could. Such was the natural response of love. But in the end, each person walks or runs a unique course and attacks the hills God allows on their paths. The hills on Debbie's Course helped me train for the half marathon. They enabled Debbie and me to build strength and endurance. Somehow, deep down, I knew the cancer hills would help me grow stronger. I prayed it would be in the area of compassion. I hoped my personal battle would help me become more compassionate to others in crisis.

Though I knew I had to run the hills alone, I did not feel alone. I pictured family and friends, near and far, cheering me on.

Yes, the hills were steep. And yes, I knew the run wouldn't be easy. But I wasn't alone.

And that gave me more strength than I could ever have imagined.

Overload

During the month following the initial diagnosis I counted over twenty appointments, procedures, and visits to doctors, nurses, and labs. Add five or six books about breast cancer, conversations, support groups, pamphlets, various e-mails, and Facebook messages, and it finally happened.

My brain hit complete overload.

I felt mentally and emotionally exhausted. All *before* surgery.

As news went out about my cancer diagnosis, our family was inundated with love and help. Our Epic Movement staff at Cru rallied around us immediately. Tommy, our director, left a voice mail saying he was fasting for me. Jenni called from Central Asia. I saved those messages in my voice mail. Sherry and Mike alerted our Pacific Southwest Cru staff friends during a staff meeting. They stopped the meeting to bring our family in prayer before God's throne. The e-mails, Facebook messages, texts, phone calls, and voice mails began to flood our home.

Wonderful. But also absolutely overwhelming.

We knew people tried to contact us because they were concerned and cared for us, but all this happened as we tried to navigate our next steps. Darrin and I would sit in the backyard to escape the constant ring of the home phone. We stopped taking calls because it became too draining to answer the same few questions from concerned friends and family. We loved them, and appreciated their concern, but we just didn't have the emotional resources to cope with it all.

Around that time Leila set up a CaringBridge account so family and friends could receive updates and prayer requests. CaringBridge is a free online journal made available for anyone facing a medical crisis. Our family and friends could receive updates and prayer requests and leave messages I could read later. The journal became a place for me to process and continue to bring people in to help us walk through the battle.

CaringBridge

I woke up this morning feeling edgy because yesterday, for really the first time since the initial news, I thought about statistics. After surgery and treatment, 80 percent remain cancer free. What about the 20 percent that don't? What if...?

Yesterday I went on my normal run and found myself crying at different points. It seems so odd that I can feel fine, work out, and still go through the days, but I have cancer growing in my body.

So, with chemo, it looks like six (what is it? servings, scoops, treatments . . . oh yeah . . .) *rounds*—gotta think boxing—of chemo.

Julia said as I was putting her down tonight, "Chemotherapy. Chemooootheraaappy. I just love saying that word."

My emotions yo-yoed from awe, gratitude, and encouragement to sadness, confusion, and anxiety . . . each day, up and down, sometimes each hour, up and down, up and down. I would read a timely Bible verse or receive a card or e-mail written with exactly what I needed to hear, and then be reminded of the plans and activities put on hold for the coming year or hear another story about how someone died from breast cancer. The breaks when cancer and my health didn't dominate my thoughts became a welcome relief and blessing.

The Thursday before surgery, Darrin and I had an appointment at the hospital. We met with a nurse who talked us through the paperwork to pre-admit me. She also covered what would happen on surgery day and asked me about my health history. The unnatural glow from the computer screen reflected off her glasses, and she looked up occasionally. Her voice, flat and monotone, matched the questions she asked. Her fingers clicked the computer keys as she filled out the form.

"Do you have issues with breathing? Asthma?"

"No."

"Do you experience bone pain? Nerve pain?"

"No. And no."

"Do you have fainting spells?"

"No."

"What medications are you on?"

"Um. I guess I take aspirin maybe five or six times a year."

On and on. Each answer was *no*, and that's when it hit me.

I thought, *I guess I love that word in a different way. I'm willing to undergo anything to reduce the chance of cancer taking me from you, Sweet Pea.*

And so today my hope level is higher than yesterday, and we are nearing a surgery date. With each appointment and decision I see God clearly going before us. Thank you for checking in and for all of your notes that I read and sometimes reread. You are impacting our lives in profound ways.

This is bizarre. I'm healthy. I still have 20/20 vision, for heaven's sake! What *am I doing here?*

But the truth was, cancer silently and steadily grew inside my body and needed to be removed and obliterated.

Surgery

The hospital allowed Darrin and the Awesome Threesome in the prep room before surgery. They took pictures. Darrin cracked some jokes. Another woman waited behind the curtain for surgery in the bed next to mine. When the hospital staff wheeled her away, the faithful four surrounded my bed and prayed for me.

"God, please give the doctors skill and wisdom."

"Please help them remove all of the cancer."

"Strengthen Darrin and the kids."

"Lord, grant Viv a smooth surgery with no complications."

"Father, give Julia special grace. She's so young and there's so much she doesn't understand."

I kept my eyes open while they prayed. I wanted to take one long look at Darrin and the Awesomes. They had been my strong support. And here they stood, surrounding me with love, covering me in prayer, still being pillars of strength for me. I felt undeserving to be loved so well. I looked down as I felt Darrin squeeze my hand and marveled at my fingernails. The nail polish hadn't chipped. As superficial as noting the condition of my nails, what it represented meant the world. Friends had come alongside us and provided meals and helped with clean up. My nails were chip-free because of the kindness of so many.

I continued to hold Darrin's hand as a nurse came in and shot some type of drug into my IV to make me woozy. It kicked in as she wheeled me down the hallway. Unknown to me, the waiting room filled with a dozen of our friends who had come to support Darrin and wait out the surgery. They set up camp, brought their laptops and snacks, and played Speed Scrabble around the coffee table.

Before the final stop at the operating room, I first had to get a shot of blue dye near the cancerous tumor. The shot caused great discomfort. The technician was curt, and he didn't seem to care how roughly jabbing the needle in my chest resulted in my tears. I lay on another cold, hard surface alone while the technician waited to make sure the dye traveled through my lymphatic system successfully.

During surgery, the doctor removed the first three blue dyed lymph nodes. This procedure, a sentinel node biopsy, would check if cancer had spread into my lymphatic system. Also during surgery she placed a port near the collarbone under my skin. This device would administer the chemotherapy drugs straight into a large vein. The port, about the size of a quarter, would also be used to draw blood to check my white blood cell count to clear me to receive chemo. Rather than running an IV line each time I visited the oncologist, the port helped the procedure move faster and smoother. But the placement of the port, instead of taking the normal ten minutes, took nearly an hour because of my small frame. This resulted in severe bruising. I could see under the bandages the next day deep purple marks that covered half my chest. I joked with Darrin, "It looks like the doctor wore army boots and stomped the port into my chest."

After the surgery, once the doctor removed and measured the tumor, the pathologist would be able to rate the stage of the cancer and the medical team would confirm the next steps of treatment.

Darrin stood by my side when I awakened in the recovery room four hours later. Earlier I had caught glimpses of the other patients in their rooms as someone wheeled me through the hallways, and I remember feeling out of place. All the patients fell into the "grandparents" category. The smell in the hallways brought back memories of visiting my ailing grandma in her nursing home.

I worried most about the kids and how they'd respond after my surgery. I wanted to see them and let them know I made it through surgery without any complications. Our friend, Jamie, picked them up from school and brought them to the hospital. When they came up to the room I could tell they were careful and cautious around the monitors and tubes. Wanting to assure them I was doing fine, I mumbled something about how my pee was blue/green now because of the dye.

A few friends popped their heads in. I weakly lifted my arm, complete with the IV line taped down, to wave. Heavily drugged and only vaguely aware I had various tubes and drains hanging out of my body, I drifted in and out of consciousness.

Darrin asked if I wanted him to stay the night, but with nowhere to sleep except a small stiff chair and the added factor of sharing a hospital room with another patient, I convinced him to return home and get rest. It had been a long day for both of us.

I spent one long night in the hospital in a room shared with an eighty-year-old woman who kept ripping her IV line out. She refused to answer questions each time the nurses came in our room to change her bloody sheet and replace her IV line. I felt too weak to get involved with what happened behind the curtain next to me. Time crawled as I floated in and out of sleep. I felt grateful whenever the time-release button allowed me to press the pain pump. When coherent I wondered, *Did they get all the cancer? Are Darrin and the kids okay?*

Darrin returned first thing in the morning to check on me. After we received clearance to check out of the hospital, a nurse entered the room with several sheets of instructions. She briefed us on how to use the pain pump, how to measure and empty the drains hanging out of me, how often to apply ice to keep the swelling down, and how to stay ahead of the pain post-surgery. I returned home with renewed appreciation for the gift of sleep in my own bed. I found baggies of frozen peas worked wonderfully in place of ice packs to help keep the swelling down because they molded to my armpits and didn't have jagged edges like ice cubes from our freezer.

The following week I shuffled around like Tim Conway on *The Carol Burnett Show*. I moved slowly, like an old man, from my bed to the bathroom and back. After a few days I could make my way all the way to the backyard. Darrin kept a yellow pad next to the bed to record the times when I took pain medication, antibiotics, and any other pills the doctor prescribed. He also used the yellow pad to record each time he measured and emptied the drains that hung from my body. The drains would be removed after the amount of blood and liquid lessened—evidence of no infection and that my body healed properly from surgery.

The kids came in after school to check on me. I tried hard to be awake to greet them. Julia popped her head in and smiled, her two front teeth missing. I could tell she had fixed her own hair. I patted the spot next to me on the bed and motioned her to join me. She clamored up, dragging her backpack behind her. The afternoon sun warmed the bed.

"Mommy, I wanted to show you my papers. I got a big sticker on my spelling test. My teacher said I did a great job."

"I'm so proud of you, Julia." I looked over her papers and stroked her long hair as Julia recounted her day. So different than her two brothers, who when asked about their days usually responded in one word answers, Julia would share in vivid detail about the conversations and activities she experienced. These moments I tucked in my heart. I didn't want to miss a single one.

Wendy, my friend from church, gave me a stuffed bear we named Vanilla Bean. As silly as it may sound, holding the bear comforted me. That, and the soft robe Leila gave me. When family and friends couldn't be around, soft things soothed my pain.

I turned a corner and felt stronger. I still had difficulty walking up and down stairs, but could walk longer, and I cut back considerably on the pain medication. I started to think life just might return to normal.

At the end of the week, the pathology report came back. I took the call from the doctor in my room.

"The pathology report says your cancer is Stage 3." My heart sank. The staging for cancer ranged from Stage 1 to Stage 4, based on the size of the tumor and whether the cancer spread to other areas of the body. Stage 4 was the worst.

"Your tumor measured four centimeters by six centimeters at the largest points."

Standing by the dresser, I looked for paper and a pen to take notes.

"I'd like you to come in and see me again this week. The lab found cancer in three spots on one of the lymph nodes we removed."

My heart sank further. I dropped my pen and covered my eyes.

"With the spread of the cancer to your lymph nodes, it looks like we will have to schedule another surgery. We have to remove all of your lymph nodes under your arm to make sure the cancer hasn't spread further."

I set up the appointment on autopilot, but inside I screamed *No! No! I can't do this again. I can't.* I pictured the hospital, the prep room, trying to swallow dry crackers at two in the morning in order to stomach the pain medication. I crumpled to the floor. The news felt unbearable.

Darrin walked into the room and helped me to the bed. I gave him the update from the doctor. He sat behind me on our bed and wrapped his arms around me and held me as I sobbed. I remember wondering, *Is this a picture of how God holds us when we struggle and suffer? His strong arms are able to contain all our fears.*

My friend from college, Mike, wrote to me that when he read on CaringBridge about the spread of the cancer and the second surgery, he almost threw his computer across the room. I didn't feel angry about the news, just overwhelmed and devastated. I didn't have words to pray, so it brought comfort to know others were praying for our family when I couldn't.

Every person on the cancer journey has a unique and personal story—similar to the way that no two people share the same spiritual journey with God or the how-I-met-my-spouse-and-knew-I-wanted-to-marry-him/her story. Each cancer story and the treatments, timetables, and issues are unique to each patient. The team of doctors tailors the treatments to the person and their specific type of cancer, the stage of cancer, the age of the patient, in the best way they know how.

I had so hoped my journey would mean no more surgeries. That I wouldn't require the more brutal treatment of radiation. But now I knew. My hopes would not be realized.

My journey now included another trip to the hospital. And once again, our friends rallied around us. They surrounded us in prayer, sent us Scripture, brought our family meals, offered to help with the kids, and wrote notes of encouragement.

We were not alone.

Three Steps Forward, Two Steps Back

The day before the second surgery, Darrin and I grabbed lunch and returned the last of the cancer books I'd borrowed from the library. As we left the library, he glanced at me. "How are you feeling about the surgery tomorrow?"

I didn't hesitate. "I'm dreading it."

"What do you mean?"

How to explain? "It's hard to not look at this second surgery as a setback rather than part of the process."

He pulled a U-turn right before we turned onto Jeronimo, the main street that took us into our neighborhood. "I want to show you something. It's not that far back. Do you know where we are going?"

CaringBridge

My hope is to be well enough and strong enough to show up for Julia's seventh birthday party Friday night. Michael's twelfth birthday is on February 16, and he wants some friends to spend the night and play football until it's dark. I want so much for the kids to be able to celebrate despite what's going on around us.

Please pray for:

- No complications from surgery so I will be strong enough to celebrate (or at least show up for) Julia and Michael's birthdays.
- Continued healing and physical strength.
- Emotional comfort for the kids.

FYI: Don't eat peas from our freezer. They have been thawing in my armpits and refrozen about a billion times.

I had no idea. This was so like Darrin. No matter what city, in a matter of days, he would discover secret ways and connect all the back roads. He observed so much more of the world than I did. I took one way to the grocery store, one way to the post office, one way to drop off the kids at school, and I stuck to those known paths. He, on the other hand, always found new ways home and would go on all these side adventures because he never asked for directions. It's part of what I loved about him—and it also drove me crazy.

He took us into the neighborhood, and we started winding around the streets. "Anything look familiar?"

"Nope."

Then I realized he brought me the back way to the ultra-mega-steep hill on Debbie's Course. I ran Debbie's Course every other day during the autumn. It became such a familiar course that I would picture running it in my mind to pass the time when I had to lie still during the PET scan and the MRIs. While the whirling and banging accosted me, I closed my eyes, slowed my breathing, and imagined leaving our front porch to run past familiar trees, houses, and other landmarks. It had been over a month since I had run in the neighborhood.

But in that moment, in the car with Darrin, when I realized where we were, my only response was streaming tears.

"This is why you're doing this tomorrow, Viv. You're going to be running these hills again one day. And this big hill, you're already halfway up it. And later on, you're going to discover new runs that you haven't even been on yet."

I wiped my face and grabbed his arm. "How did you know I needed to see this hill?" We stopped at the top, silent tears flowing, and took in the view.

It brought hope and perspective I hadn't even realized I lacked.

I feared the surgery. I didn't want the pain pump, drains, pain medications, iced peas, antibiotics, and especially the emotional toll it would take on Darrin and the kids. But the view at the top of the hill stayed with me.

Three steps forward, two steps back, but still *forward* . . . so onward we would go.

Love Is a Verb

The recovery from the second surgery went smoother in some ways, but the pain was more difficult to manage. From the initial meeting at my Starbucks, at least once a week the Awesome Three-some would gather in our living room to check in on me and pray. Debbie set up a sign-up schedule for meals. Leila became the communication hub. Kelly was the information synthesizer. My parents came to town, and before they left they bought us a new refrigerator. We placed the old one in our garage. We gave our friends the garage code so they could leave meals in the fridge when convenient. Missy, Shirley, and Joanne—friends from our home church—set up a grocery-shopping schedule. Most days Leila visited after her boys went to school and helped with anything and everything. All the help from so many people opened up space for me to rest and heal so I would be strong enough to begin chemotherapy.

> **CaringBridge**
>
> Getting ready to head over to the hospital to check in. Wanted you to know that I'm feeling peaceful, rested, and hungry. I know it's because you've been praying.

Thankfully I was able to show up for my daughter's seventh birth-day party—and it was such a balm to see so many people I hadn't seen since before surgery. Simone and Abby, moms from Julia's elementary school, took care of every detail and threw a wonderful party. I still had drains hanging out of my body under my jacket and felt loopy from the strong pain medication, but I felt it important to show up for Julia's sake. Since I'd missed her Christmas party, I resolved to attend every significant celebration. Cancer might have turned my life upside down, but I would not allow it to rob me of memories with the kids.

I left early to rest in the car, but felt incredible gratitude for such good friends who loved Julia and our family. Julia's party showed me that love is a verb. Not a casually thrown around emotional word anymore—action and sacrifice demonstrated love lived out.

Two days later, we celebrated Michael's twelfth birthday. He invited a group of friends over for a backyard football game, pizza, cake, candy, and play-till-your-eyeballs-fall-out video games. I fell asleep smiling in our bedroom across the hall from the TV room, listening to the sixth-grade boys sing classic rock songs to the Rock Band Wii game. Another attempt at living out life as normal as possible for the kids.

A few days later, Lisa, with her gorgeous, sassy red hair and bright smile, drove the hour from Riverside to our house to help out. She and I became Anne-of-Green-Gables kindred friends when our oldest sons were still infants. Over the years, through moves to different cities, through heartache and job changes, overalls and the "Rachel" haircut from *Friends*, parenting challenges and late-night talks, God knit our hearts together. Lisa, like the Awesome Threesome had in previous weeks, jumped in and attacked the loads and loads of laundry, cleaned up, and cooked a delicious meal. Her cheerful attitude and willing heart refreshed me. From the time of diagnosis, Lisa wore a special silver bracelet to help remind her to pray for me.

We might have been distant in miles, but in our hearts—in living out love as a verb—we were as close as could be.

Being Royalty

My greasy and stringy hair needed washing. Since the surgery scars hadn't healed, and tubes still hung out of my body, I could not take showers. I watched, fighting laughter, as Darrin constructed the perfect combination of patio cushions and beach towels on the bathroom floor. It took several attempts but he finally arranged them so my head rested comfortably over the rim of the sliding shower door. The cushions and towels covered the original 1968 ugly, orange-brown tiles.

The only attempt at updating our bathroom came years earlier when we peeled off the faded blue and white flower wallpaper and applied paint over the water damage on the walls. It took two tries. The first time I couldn't place why I didn't like the color. Kelly came over, took one look, and nailed it: "It's public-restroom green." So I painted over public restroom green with a slightly better color.

Darrin and I had worked on improving our home, piece by piece, replacing the windows, the flooring in the entryway and living room, the water heater, the deck. But we soon realized home improvement for an old house would be a never-ending job. We had updated the other bathrooms, but the little one attached to our master bedroom remained essentially the same. A small sink that leaked water onto the counter when the hot water was turned on, an old toilet with a flimsy plastic seat, water damage on the ceiling, rusty medicine cabinet, and an old sliding door for the walk-in shower. So much like how I felt.

I reclined on the cushions. Darrin, dressed in his swim trunks, stood in the shower adjusting the water temperature.

"Sooooo, how's the water? Too hot? Too cold?"

"It's perfect."

He smiled at my answer.

I was prone to exaggerate and look at life in black and white. I would ask him after a meal, "Did that hit the spot?" He would comment, "That's so either/or. Either the meal hits perfection or it doesn't. The spot. What exactly is the spot?"

He snapped open my shampoo bottle. The familiar fragrance brought surprising comfort. I looked into Darrin's eyes as he tenderly washed my hair. He smiled, cracked some jokes, dotted my nose with soap bubbles. I exhaled slowly and relaxed, taking in the moment. I couldn't recall another time when I felt so vulnerable and so taken care of. Though the bathroom was small and old, I felt like a queen there.

This is what "in sickness and in health" meant. I took a snapshot in my mind. And over the months, I filled the mental album as I watched Darrin live out our marriage vows. Photos of when he gently wiped sticky hospital tape off my arms, comforted me when I cried, cheered me on with each milestone, held my hand during doctor's appointments, and helped me when I threw up in the backyard from a bad combo of pain and a cocktail of medications.

Darrin's shoulders were so broad I could stand behind him and be completely hidden. After the surgery, we switched sides of the bed and I slept with seven pillows all propped up this way and that, which left him a grand total of eight inches of sleep space. Not that he slept much, as he would empty and take measurements from my drains or exchange ice packs or baggies of frozen peas or meds every few hours.

The mixture of blood and body fluid that filled the drains didn't repel him. In college, after a powerful conversion experience, Darrin decided to pursue vocational Christian ministry rather than become a medical doctor. Calm and steady in crisis, gifted with incredible fine motor skills, he watched in fascination the emergency C-section of Jonathan's birth. Noticing him lift one of the drains to the light to read the measurement line and fill in the chart on the yellow pad on the nightstand, I thought to myself, *He would have made an excellent doctor.*

"Look, Viv, the amount is slowly going down. Less today than yesterday." He left the room to dump out the contents in the bathroom. From the bathroom he asked, "Does it feel any different? Can you feel when the liquid comes out?"

"No. I can't tell. It's surprising how much blood fills the drains. I can't wait until we finally get to the level where they can take these tubes out so I can take a shower."

Back by the bedside he squeezed the air out of the drains and reattached them to the tubes hanging out of my body. Over time the drain would fill. And the process would begin all over again.

Everywhere he went, people asked him how I was doing, and over and over he answered questions and relayed messages to me. Messenger, narcotic dispenser, post-surgery medical overseer, and hospital bill decipherer—all these new roles he took on without complaint.

We didn't and still don't have the perfect marriage or kids. The health challenges stirred up our existing marital issues in new ways, even amplifying them at times. I had spent much of our marriage playing the role of cruise director, trying to keep everyone happy. I tried especially hard to anticipate what Darrin wanted or needed without asking him. Not wanting to disappoint anyone, I learned to avoid conflict by lying about what I truly thought or felt. Whenever I experienced Darrin's disapproval or anger, I would emotionally shut down and move into a pattern of avoidance. Darrin didn't find conflict threatening, but when avoided his response would move from agitation to anger. His anger would repel me further into avoidance—a vicious cycle. But through the ups and downs, our inevitable fights over the same issues, times of misunderstanding, defensiveness, and blame, Darrin committed himself to demonstrating unconditional love.

He was, and is, a hero in every sense.

Two Months

Two months had passed since I learned I had cancer. Two months. Honestly, it felt like two years. Waiting in the line of cars to pick up the kids from school I thought, *Life still goes on for everyone around me but my life has come to a complete halt. All of my plans are put on hold.*

Two months and I struggled emotionally because I felt worn out and tired of not feeling well, of dealing with various levels of pain and discomfort, of physical limitations, of not being able to drive or take a shower or run or wave my arms around and just physically feel good. I felt like it had been *forever* since I felt well.

Nighttime was the hardest. I struggled most with body aches. My mind raced at night. All of my fears, all the what-ifs I beat back during the day, would tumble out unrestrained at night. By the end of the day I felt raw and exposed, and everything amplified at night. I fought going to sleep because I didn't want to wake up and face cancer, realizing it wasn't a bad dream.

But cancer was real.

And it stunk.

4
the fight is on

Here is what I am commanding you to do. Be strong and brave.
Do not be terrified. Do not lose hope. I am the LORD your God.
I will be with you everywhere you go.

Joshua 1:9 (NIrV)

My oncologist was, in a word, *Wow.* Truly brilliant, humble, personable, thoughtful, warm, kind, and knowledgeable. I really, really liked her. Around 70 percent of her patients were women battling breast cancer. Her smile and hugs warmed the otherwise on-the-cooler-side examination room. She sat down in front of her computer and pulled up my file, double clicked the mouse. Pushing her chair with wheels she positioned herself closer to us as she cheerfully announced, "I went over your pathology reports. Based on these reports, your prognosis is excellent! The secondary surgery shows no further spreading of cancer in the lymph nodes."

Wonderful, wonderful, grateful-tear-producing news.

Karyn, the head oncology nurse, entered the room with a thick green folder and pulled up the chair. "Okay, don't be overwhelmed. This will be a lot of information at one time. If you have questions or forget something, this is my direct number. You can leave me a message anytime and I will get back to you." She opened the green folder. "Your chemo regimen will be three different drugs." She wrote in capital letters on the first page *TAC.*

"Taxotere, Adriamycin, and Cytoxan. Now, these pages here explain what the side effects may be. Not everyone responds the same way. Just like what's printed on the side of a box of aspirin, not everyone experiences all of the side effects."

"So maybe I won't lose my hair?"

"No, unfortunately you will lose all your hair. These drugs attack all fast growing cells, which includes hair cells." I nodded but inside I felt the tantrum of a toddler. I dreaded the thought of losing my hair.

She continued explaining the contents of the folder, over-the-counter medications I would take, and the timeline for the chemo treatments. "Do you have any questions?"

"Well, we have some friends who got engaged in Japan last summer. Our whole family took part in the proposal. They asked Julia to be a flower girl in their May wedding in Hawaii. It's been one of Julia's lifelong dreams to be a flower girl. Can we still go?"

Karyn smiled and flipped the calendar ahead and counted back. "Your best days will be right before you start another round. Your body has three weeks between each round to repair. Looks like we can time it for you to attend."

I took the calendar and flipped to June. "This will work out really well. The final round of chemo will take place after Michael's sixth-grade promotion."

Karyn asked me as she handed me the folder, "Does your insurance cover Emend?"

I looked at Darrin. He shrugged his shoulders.

"Find out if it does. This drug is worth its weight in gold for dealing with nausea." Karyn's dark brown eyes were steady and full of compassion. She decided to set up a two-hour hydration treatment for the day after each chemo treatment. I was already scheduled to return to the office to get a shot in my stomach of a medication called Neulasta. The drug would help jump-start my bone marrow's white blood cell production. The hydration treatment involved hooking the port up to a bag of saline and electrolytes that would replenish and help flush out my system. "I don't set this up for everyone, but my gut tells me this is something that will help you, so I'm going with my gut."

I think her gut must've been God prompting her. Over and over I saw divine intervention preparing, providing, and directing each step of our journey. I left more informed, with many of my preconceived notions about chemo cleared up. I pictured being bedridden for months, throwing up all the time, in a gloomy, depressing, dark office for weeks at a time, cold, bald, sad . . . oh-so-bleak (start the violins playing). I was way off—except for the bald part. Situated across the street from a lake, the chemotherapy office had ceiling-to-floor glass windows. Comfortable leather recliners lined the infusion area that overlooked a relaxing view of the water.

Yet as my body grew stronger, and the date to begin chemo neared, I found myself turning inside and emotionally shutting down. I didn't know what to expect or how my body would tolerate the chemo cocktail of Taxotere, Adriamycin, and Cytoxan. My oncologist wanted all three to be given simultaneously to get the best results because each chemo drug attacked the cells in different ways (e.g., one kept cells from dividing, one killed cancer cells). If my body couldn't handle this mix, they would administer two medicines together and give the last chemo medicine separately, which would lengthen the time in chemotherapy. Because they considered me young, the doctor thought my body could handle taking all three together.

I had no way of knowing how my body would react to chemo.

Let's face it . . . chemo unnerved me.

Chemo Boxing

Darrin observed I worried most about chemo and losing my hair—more than my fear of surgery, even the second one. Both chemo and losing my hair seemed like longer processes. I took to life like a sprinter, going at fast speeds for short amounts of time and then fizzling and burning out. I hadn't learned to be consistent, paced, steadfast. Chemo would take the longest of all my phases of treatment with no way to hurry the process. Six rounds of a three-combination chemo cocktail every three weeks for the next four months.

The hair thing, well, it just seemed so glaring and obvious and out there, instantly labeling me *cancer patient.* Not ashamed about having cancer, I still found myself identifying with pregnant teenage girls who go away for a year to have the baby and return when their bodies are back to normal. Part of me wanted to disappear and not be seen until all my hair grew back and life returned to normal, even though I knew nothing would ever really be normal again. I felt fragile, vulnerable, and emotionally not up to dealing with people's comments like, "It doesn't even look like a wig!" or "You look great." What if strangers stared at me, or worse, people avoided looking, looked away, or felt sorry for me? I didn't want people's pity.

Round 1 (Ding-Ding!)

The steroid I took the night before my first round kept me from restful sleep. I experienced hot flashes for the first time. Several times during the night, I woke up drenched in sweat, which left my sheets and pillow damp. Now I understood the hot flash jokes I'd heard at a women's retreat months back.

Kelly created a meds chart so I could keep track of the nine different pills I had to take before, during, and after the treatment. The next morning, after taking multiple pills and checking off boxes, I carefully applied the numbing cream over my port and covered that cream with plastic wrap. I found a small lid a little larger than the port while rummaging through the medicine cabinet. I placed it over the plastic wrap and let my bra strap hold the plastic lid in place. The port, about the size of a quarter, felt awkward and uncomfortable, especially when my seat belt rested directly over it. Tank top straps also rubbed against the round bulge of foreign material. The port served as a constant reminder I had cancer.

I hated it.

Karyn had explained that, since this would be my first treatment, I would probably stay in the doctor's office all day. In preparation I packed a sage-colored super soft blanket, a travel pillow, warm socks, snacks, and all sorts of books and papers in a bag that could have been an airplane carry-on. We stopped at a Subway near our house to pick up deli sandwiches for lunch.

Darrin joked as he carried my bags through the parking lot, "Looks like I'm your personal Sherpa." It appeared as though we were moving in and setting up home. Of course I used only the blanket, pillow, and socks. Everything else stayed in my bag. Just like when we travel by air.

I settled into one of the leather recliners, while Karyn toted the metal pole with wheels. For some reason seeing the contraption made the experience feel more serious. I'd seen hospital scenes in TV shows and movies with close-ups of the metal pole and the hanging plastic bags along with a constant drip from the bag to the catheter tubing.

The numbing cream worked. A round disc with a metal needle snapped in place to the port with very little discomfort. Karyn first pushed some saline through the needle to clear out the port. I tasted the solution instantly in my nasal cavity. Next she connected the port to the bags of cold liquids. Several clear bags of saline and chemo drugs, each marked with black Sharpie, hung from the metal pole. The red stuff, Adriamycin, was so strong and toxic it would be administered each time by hand through a large plastic syringe into the catheter tubing. I read that if the medication accidentally leaked out of my veins into the surrounding tissue, the skin and muscles would be severely damaged.

We began around 10:30 a.m. and finished by 2:30 p.m. Darrin sat on a chair next to the window, facing the recliner across from me. I moved from talkative, jazzed up from the steroid, to sleepy from the Benadryl—also included in the liquid mixture going into my veins.

While checking the fluid level on one of the bags, I asked one of the nurses how she chose the oncology field.

"I had a mom who died from breast cancer."

"Oh. I am so sorry."

"Well, the sad thing was she refused to get chemotherapy. She chose one of those homeopathic routes. I think if she had gone through chemo she would probably still be here. So I figured if I couldn't help my mom I would help others receive chemotherapy treatment."

I'm sure some cancer patients found success from homeopathic routes, but hearing her story, I quietly prayed a prayer of thanksgiving for the opportunity to receive chemo.

After another hour passed, I asked another nurse how she ended up helping cancer patients.

"I had a step-dad who died from a brain tumor." Tears filled her eyes. "His death marked my life and I knew I wanted to invest the rest of my life helping cancer patients."

Throughout my cancer treatment, the nurses impressed me most. I appreciated my doctors, but the nurses were the heart and hands of my healing journey. They answered my questions, returned my calls, offered suggestions, and walked closely beside me. They helped me know what to expect, what to look out for; they were the accessible ones, the personal lifeline when treatment felt confusing or uncertain. They possessed the extraordinary intellect to understand the complexity of the human body, and they balanced their knowledge with compassion and the ability to move toward people and into their pain.

To celebrate the end of our first round, Darrin took me to my favorite frozen yogurt place. I fell asleep when we returned home. The next day I went in for the hydration treatment and the Neulasta shot. They injected the shot into my padded belly area. I turned away and stared at a spot on the wall and used Lamaze breathing to help me relax.

Over the weekend I felt queasy and achy. No food sounded good, so I had difficulty figuring out what to eat to calm my upset stomach. I continued to adjust to hot flashes and felt yucky overall.

Very yucky.

I had a hard time not feeling sorry for myself. I intentionally determined to swim upstream against the fibers in my Asian DNA of not rocking the boat or inconveniencing others. Darrin, half Japanese, who grew up in a predominantly Japanese town, Hilo, Hawaii, taught me about Japanese culture. Growing up with so few Asians around me in Colorado, I assumed Asians were all the same. While cultural similarities were true in all Asian cultures like honoring elders, the importance of group over the individual, and indirect communication, each Asian culture had its own unique traits. I thought about how a Japanese restaurant, with the quiet music and perfect food presentation had little resemblance to a loud Chinese restaurant serving dim-sum with the waiters pushing carts and yelling out the names of the dishes over the din of the crowd.

I learned from Darrin and my other Japanese American friends about the Japanese phrase *Sho ga nai*, which translates "Nothing can be done about it." In other words, it was honorable to swallow our suffering and resist help from others. The purpose of this posture? To not lose face and put others out. And while I could understand the nobility in not troubling others, I kept remembering the Asian Martha Stewart. I didn't want to isolate like she did. I didn't want to swallow my suffering because honestly, the challenges before us grew bigger than I could handle alone. No, I wanted to cut a new path. I tried to not minimize or talk myself out of how I felt. And I decided to welcome the help of others.

CaringBridge

I'm getting ready to crash. Got my star pajamas on (thanks Pacific Southwest Cru staff moms) and took half a pill that will help with my queasy stomach and knock me out so I hope to sleep better tonight. Last night one of the steroid medicines kept me tossing and turning with hot flashes most of the night.

The first chemo treatment went smoothly. Experienced a little difficulty with getting the port going in the beginning, but it all worked out and I didn't experience any complications during the chemo treatment.

The nurse introduced me to a lady who was on her final round of chemo. All of us in the room celebrated with her. I look forward to the day when it will be me. One round down, five to go.

I got home and took a nap and woke up and then took a walk around the whole block with Julia and Darrin. It's the longest I've

I also arranged my life so I'd have one thing to look forward to each day. I only had the energy for that one thing, though my capacity would eventually grow as my body regained strength after being taken all the way down. Saturday's one thing was wig shopping with Audrey and the Awesomes. They watched and laughed as I tried on an assortment of different wigs, colors, styles. I tried on long blonde wigs, short curly wigs, wigs with bangs, wigs with highlights—my chance to break out and try something wild. But in the end, nothing at the shop suited me, so I ordered a sassy wig named *Shasta* from a catalog. From that day on I signed my name Shasta on my e-mails to the Awesomes whenever I felt extra sassy.

After the first round of chemo I felt groggy and queasy, and my mouth had a disgusting coat of I don't know what . . . chemo chemicals that never went away. I slept with a wad of sugarless gum on the roof of my mouth. Each time I awoke from pain or hot flashes, I chewed the gum to get rid of the metallic taste. I kept crackers near my bed, like I'd done when I was pregnant. The one thing I found comfort drinking: Grandma Faye's (Kelly's mother-in-law) miso soup with rice. Kelly brought over a large plastic container made with love and sent from her mother-in-law. The miso swirled around the warm broth, and cubes of tofu and pieces of seaweed were seasoned with just the right amount of salt.

By Monday I had rehearsed a thousand times in my head my resignation call to Karyn. It went something like this, "Hello Karyn. Yeah, it's nice to hear your voice, too. My weekend? Well, not so good. I just wanted to let you know I'm never coming back. Don't get me wrong. I really like you. And I like the office staff, the view of the water. But chemo? No thank you. I'm done. I wanted to call to let you know it's not you; it's me. That's all. Buh-bye."

walked since surgery! I had to take a few breaks along the way, but being out felt good.

I started feeling queasy a little bit ago so I need to get to bed.

Thank you so much for praying. I went in feeling supernatural peace and really felt lifted up in prayer. Now the next few days will reveal how my body will respond to all of the stuff coursing around my bloodstream.

For now, good night.

When we finally did connect, her compassionate voice encouraged me to hang on a little longer.

"By the end of the week you'll feel better. Really."

"Really? Are you sure?"

"Everything you've described is very normal. Nothing is out of the ordinary. It's going to take some time for your body to recover. But you will feel better in a few more days. Promise."

"Okay, I'll hang on a little longer."

She was right.

5

the wall

With your help I can advance against a troop; with my God I can scale a wall.

2 Samuel 22:30 (NIV)

Running a marathon hadn't been on any lifetime bucket list I'd put together. I found no appeal in 26.2 miles of guaranteed physical pain. I knew, however, many people who had run marathons. On a long flight, I watched part of a movie called *Run, Fatboy, Run* about a man who ran a marathon in England. During the marathon scene, the man ran on and on through the streets of England. By nightfall he arrived at the wall. From what I understand, the wall is the part in a marathon when a runner's body simply shuts down and refuses to go any farther. Successfully navigating the wall determined whether the runner would be able to complete the marathon.

In the movie, the man imagined a literal brick wall and had to mentally break through to finish the race.

Now I could relate. I neared the part of the cancer race marathon that represented my personal wall. While my wall wasn't physically painful, it felt difficult, devastating, hard, challenging. Definitely wall-like.

My wall? Losing my hair.

Karyn went through the calendar counting out the days to total about three weeks. "March 19 or 20 is when your hair will start falling out. It will begin with a tingling sensation on your scalp, kind of like someone pulling on your hair."

"Will it hurt?"

"No, but you will be able to tell something is different."

I continued to feel physically stronger and stronger, walking farther and longer—but my focus returned over and over again to the looming date.

I spent time thinking through why this part of the journey was so challenging for me. One quote I read from a cancer book, *There's No Place Like Hope* by Vickie Girard, helped me understand:

"Hair loss allows our illness to enter the room before our name."

Up to this point, except for not having as much range of motion in my arms and being physically weaker and slower, no one from the outside could discern I battled cancer.

Hair loss would be a constant reminder—to me and anyone who saw me—that I didn't battle the flu or have my gall bladder removed.

I tried to play over in my mind what it would feel like to wake up and see my head bald, or to catch my reflection in a window without hair.

Over the years I've learned that unexpected trials and stress serve as a refining heat that draws unresolved issues to the surface. I saw this in my marriage, with my extended family, and in my own life. I also began to see how my cancer battle tapped into unresolved grief in others. It surprised me how people who I thought would be supportive just . . . disappeared. And people I never expected to do so came alongside and entered the fray.

Eventually, I noticed that the fear of losing my hair played into an ongoing theme woven throughout my life: wanting to fit in.

As a child, I lived as a minority. We lived in a breathtaking part of the United States: Boulder, Colorado. I grew up looking at the Flatiron Mountains and walking on the wacky Pearl Street Mall. I relished four seasons, pine-scented air, the feel of sandstone, and aspen leaves in the fall. Though I loved growing up in Boulder, I struggled with being a minority—one of the few Asian Americans in town.

As a little girl, I scanned the shelves at the toy store looking for a doll that resembled me. Disney princesses and Barbies looked like all the girls I saw around me, but none of them matched my black hair and small eyes. Every heroine in the stacks of books I read from the library, every lead in the plays, movies, and television shows, every option given for biography reports in school reinforced in my mind that I didn't fit in. No one looked anything like me. No one lived in my world. Even though I was born in Wisconsin and spoke perfect English, strangers would think, and still think to this day, I came from another country. Classmates who overheard me speak Chinese with my grandmother would run up during recess pulling their eyelids tight and would tease me yelling, "Hey! Ching-ching-chang-chang-chong! Tell me what I just said in Japanese."

In high school I tried everything I knew to be all American— cheerleader, junior class president, and president of different clubs. But no matter what I did, deep down I knew I would never date the captain of the football team or be nominated for a homecoming court because of my appearance. I flipped through *Seventeen* magazines trying to figure out how to apply eye makeup without a double eyelid. But I couldn't escape the truth.

I looked different.

What I most wanted? To fit in.

I lived in two worlds. At home we spoke Chinese and ate foods like sea cucumber and winter melon with chopsticks. We ate rice at almost every meal. My favorite snack foods included roasted watermelon seed, dried cuttle fish, and preserved plums surrounded by three layers of wrappers with a seed in the middle. My grandmother lived with us and packed my school lunches. My friends had Ding-Dongs, but I would hide behind my Cinderella lunch box lid, embarrassed as I ate my Chinese ground pork sandwich. The sitcoms on TV, even the commercials, looked nothing like my home life. I knew TV life wasn't real, but even my friends' holiday celebrations, home decorations, and family dynamics looked nothing like what I experienced in my home. Outside the home, I pursued anything I could think of to find the magic combination that would help me feel like I belonged.

Going bald resurfaced the struggle. It highlighted and underscored how once again I would look different. People would make assumptions, outside of my control, based on how I looked.

Darrin grew up in Hawaii in an Asian-majority culture. He worked hard to learn and understand my struggles even though they weren't his own. I realized later on that, though I never dated the captain of the football team in high school, as God would have it, I ended up *marrying* him! Which made it that much more profound when Darrin came to me one day and offered to shave his head to go bald with me so I wouldn't be alone.

Settling onto our lumpy couch to join me as I flipped through TV channels, Darrin took my hand. "Hey, so I was thinking. How would you feel if I shaved my head bald?"

I dropped the remote control to the floor. "Really? You would do that?"

"Sure, Viv. We could be like the Coneheads in the old *Saturday Night Live* skits."

"You don't need to do that for me."

"I want to. I want to support you any way I can. I know the going bald part has been a big struggle. But I won't do it if it makes you feel uncomfortable. So what do you think?"

I threw my arms around his neck, tears filling my eyes. "I can't believe you would do that for me. Yes. It would mean so much. Yes. Let's be Coneheads together."

Darrin's decision to daily shave his head and be bald alongside me brought comfort to the hardest part of my cancer journey. And it gave me what I'd longed for all those years.

A sense I wasn't the only one.

Coming Out

I walked Debbie's Course with renewed determination. I no longer needed to stop to rest, even on the ultra-mega-steep hill, driven by a need to know I could walk all of it before I hit the wall. I thought if I could be physically strong enough for the hills, then somehow I would be strong enough emotionally for the looming wall. During different points, tears blurred my vision. I reflected on how different life had become. I thought about the wall and marveled at the peace I felt knowing people prayed for me and that God answered those prayers. I felt literally *lifted* up as I walked past the familiar driveways and landmarks I'd come to know so well.

My heart had been expanded through battling breast cancer. Some people were born with God-given gifts of compassion and empathy. Not me. But I noticed a change . . . when I heard of others who needed prayer for physical healing or who struggled with chronic pain, my heart softened. In the same way I had connected with others over the challenges in our family from food allergies, I now could relate with a whole new group of people dealing with medical challenges.

Leila accompanied me to a physical therapy appointment a few days later. I had been seeing Gina, an incredible lymphedema specialist. Her name had been mentioned repeatedly in different circles when I attended breast-cancer support groups. Her experience, tender heart, and joyful spirit made me look forward to my physical therapy appointments. I increased the range of motion in my arm, and this helped in the hope department.

After the appointment, Leila and I went to a little wig shop for cancer patients. Leila has an eye for style. She can pull together colors, patterns, and textures like magic. I, on the other hand, lack the eye. Left to myself, I stand in the middle of stores frozen like a raccoon caught in a flashlight beam. Leila used her magic powers and picked out fun hats and scarfs and head wraps for me. We returned home to find our friend Lucy had left a box full of beautiful silk scarves for me to borrow.

Instead of letting my hair fall out in massive clumps and going through a mangy-dog-hair phase, I decided I, and not the chemo, would determine when I went bald. Loose strands of hair came out every time I ran my fingers through my hair now. The tingly sensation on my scalp began. The hair in the drain after my showers looked like after pregnancy hair loss—times five.

It had begun.

I asked Jesslyn to come over to my house for the head shaving.

All Gone

The first thing that popped into my head when my eyes opened that morning was, "Today's the day. Wait. Did Darrin really shave his head yesterday?" I looked over at him sleeping, noting his handsome face and bald head. He had buzzed his hair army short after dinner and then shaved it bald. Okay, not a dream. Bring it on!

The Awesome Threesome and their families and my friend Kierstin came over for a potluck with our family to simply be with us as Jesslyn skillfully and gently buzzed, then shaved, my head. I wanted the time to be upbeat. I wanted to include Jonathan, Michael, and Julia in this part of the journey. Rather than dread the milestone, I wanted to bring others into it. Conversation, food, and laughter filled the air. It felt like just another dinner party we were hosting.

After dinner Leila's seven-year-old son, Micah, stopped me in the hallway outside our bedroom door. "Aunty Viv, I wanted to read you something. I got it at school."

I knelt down and looked into his eyes. He pulled a strip of blue paper out of his jeans pocket. He unfolded the paper and read the verse to me: "You, O Lord, keep my lamp burning; my God turns my darkness into light. With your help I can advance against a troop; with my God I can scale a wall. As for God, His way is perfect; the word of the Lord is flawless. He is a shield for all who take refuge in Him. Psalm 18:28–30."

I put both my hands on his shoulders. "Micah, those verses are perfect. Thank you so much. It's just what I needed to hear. Seriously. Wow."

He smiled and handed me the wrinkled blue paper. I blinked back tears as I thanked him again and hugged him tight.

Everyone gathered around, sitting on the couches and standing against

CaringBridge

I'm bald now!

My head feels sensitive and tingly, and I feel cold. When I look in the mirror, I'm struck with how shiny my scalp looks—a blinding brightness. I love the various hats and scarves and my wig. Jesslyn gave the thumbs up, too, and said, "That wig is the same cut I gave you!" Tonight I go to bed with a heart full of gratitude at the incredible love and support that has been shown me both tonight and all the way leading up to this point.

My hair is gone, but my heart is full . . . and I'm really okay with how things are right now. It's much better than I imagined it was going to be.

Thanks for checking in and for all of your words of encouragement and prayers. Thank you. Thank you. Thank you.

the wall. Right there in the middle of the living room, surrounded by people I loved, the transformation took place. I felt incredibly loved and supported. No tears shed (except for welling up when Micah read to me) and tremendous peace in my heart. Everything I wanted and needed.

And the wall came crashing down. And the hair fell to the ground. No match for love in action.

6

the chemo life

We also exult in our tribulations, knowing that tribulation brings about perseverance; and perseverance, proven character; and proven character, hope; and hope does not disappoint, because the love of God has been poured out within our hearts.

Romans 5:3–5

As the weeks marched on, the effects of chemo continued. My skin became dry and flaky. I noticed changes in pigmentation around my eyes. Dark spots that looked like makeup smudges appeared under the outer corners of my eyes. My toenails and fingernails felt tender and started turning gray. Deep ridges covered the surface of my thumbnails and big toe. I continued to lose my hair. Patches of stubble grew back for the first few weeks following the head shaving. After I rubbed lotion on my scalp one night, my hands came away with tiny black hair stubble. I rinsed my hands in the sink and reapplied lotion, only to find more stubble covering my hands. I grabbed a hand towel and wiped my head over and over. When I finished my head was almost completely stubble-free.

I tried to imagine what it would have been like to have each of those pieces of stubble be long hair. I felt helpless and out-of-control. But watching the stubble swirl around the sink as it washed down the drain also felt matter of fact. The chemo medicines were at work, wiping out all fast-growing cells, including hair cells. But more important, the toxic medicines attacked any lingering cancer cells.

I needed regular reminders chemo was *not* my enemy, the cancer was. When discouragement attacked, I thought about why I elected to enter the ring for chemo boxing. In the movie *Cinderella Story* Russell Crowe played a boxer during the Depression. After he won his matches, an interviewer asked what motivated him to fight. He replied, "For milk."

His family had lost everything. First they sold their jewelry and watches, and eventually they lost their home and had to move into a run-down basement. His wife stood at the sink of their old, dark, sparse living quarters, adding water to their milk to make it stretch. She divided one slice of baloney for the family during a meal. This husband and father would do anything to provide for his family. He knew exactly why he boxed.

Why did *I* fight?

I fought for the chance to grow old with Darrin, and someday be like our friends Rollo and Barbara—an amazing couple in our small group, married longer than anyone else I knew. They were great-grandparents! Each of those words: great and grand and parents described them well. In their mid-eighties, full of sagacity and *fun*, they held hands as they flew down a huge blow-up slide at one of our church potlucks. After that brilliant display of unexpected *incredible*, I knew I wanted to be near them and become like them.

CaringBridge

My sister-in-law, Esther, came to visit from Hawaii over the weekend. It was so great to be with her as she jumped into life with us, with school drop-offs and pick-ups, football games (Michael's and the ones on TV), Uno games with Julia, and so on. We were watching a movie and I remember thinking, *It's so great to have Esther here. She is such a joy to be around.* And then it occurred to me that I have cancer. I had forgotten for a time, and then it hit me all over again. It still seems so surreal. I have to say, the

Rollo and Barbara emulated strength, love, and a lifetime of working through the hard times and relishing the good times. Darrin and I had a long way to go to be like them, but seeing a couple who had remained faithful to each other and to their wedding vows for sixty-plus years stirred profound hope in my heart.

I also fought to show up for the big and small events in Jonathan's, Michael's, and Julia's lives. I fought so I would be around to help them learn to navigate their emotions, their relationships, their disappointments. I fought so I could help them learn about God and how He made them. I wanted to be around to celebrate each milestone. I wanted to toast with sparkling apple cider who they were and what they accomplished.

Michael, when he was around six, grabbed my hand and walked me out into the backyard. "Mom, let's play soccer!" I turned around to go get my shoes and he pointed to the foldout chair. "No. You sit here and cheer for me while I kick the ball."

little breaks when I'm not thinking about my health have been a blessing.

The meals have continued to be such a blessing because it's opened up more time to take care of things, be with family, and not have to go through the "What am I going to make for dinner?" mental anguish. It's still true . . . my favorite food is anything I don't have to make.

Thank you for your continued prayers, love, and concern. We have really sensed God's peace and protection over us.

I reconnected with a high school friend on Facebook, and she shared a quote that sums it up well: "Live your life in such a way that Satan says, when your feet hit the floor as you wake up for the day, "Oh no! She's awake!"

Thanks for battling with us and for us.

It didn't matter if thousands of nameless faces sat in the crowds cheering them on, having mom in the stands mattered. I pictured each milestone: birthdays, driver's licenses, graduations, weddings . . .

I fought for the chance to have a front-row seat.

That's what I held to every time I had to enter the ring for another treatment. That I loved my family and wanted to be there for them—and though chemo was a high price to pay, it was worth it.

No Nose Hairs

I first heard about Del Cerro Elementary School from Debbie when she moved from Colorado. She had researched schools and moved into a neighborhood near some of the best public schools in Mission Viejo, California. Since our firstborn Jonathan had a fall birthday, Darrin and I talked about whether to send him to school early or wait so he could be one of the older students in his class. Academically he was ready, so we sent him to the school in our neighborhood to start kindergarten. It surprised me to learn that several boys in his kindergarten class were turning seven and Jonathan had barely turned five. When we learned Del Cerro was a GATE (Gifted and Talented Education) regional site, we submitted the necessary paperwork to transfer schools. School officials wouldn't notify us his status until late August.

At least weekly, while we waited to hear, I found myself driving over to the street overlooking the school near Debbie's house. My arms would rest on the steering wheel as my eyes looked out over the school, playground equipment, and grass fields. I tried to picture Jonathan as a student hanging his backpack on the hooks outside the classroom doors. I prayed out loud as I sat in my car and asked God for an opening at the school. When we finally received the letter that he got in, I cried grateful tears. Once Jonathan started at Del Cerro it paved the way for Michael and Julia to also attend.

The teachers at Del Cerro were fantastic. They loved teaching and they loved the kids in their classes. When one of our favorite first-grade teachers moved away before Julia could be in her class, I worried. But as God would have it, Julia was put in Sandy Leifer's class. Sandy had been diagnosed with Stage 4 breast cancer the year before. I later learned we had the same oncologist and surgical oncologist.

Of all the years, of all the teachers, God knew.

God placed Julia with the teacher she most needed—one who understood firsthand what was happening with us at home. God knew Julia would need to see Mrs. Leifer's cheerful, warrior-in-pink, survivor smile every morning. Sandy was not only a gift to Julia, but also to me. She answered my questions. She shared resources and books, and sent a steady stream of notes and cards of encouragement throughout our year. Sandy prepared me for no nose hairs from chemo.

Frankly, such a thing had never crossed my mind.

Basically it meant my nose would run without pause or filter if I cried, had a cold, or experienced allergies. I kept forgetting my tissues, so I was rarely prepared for those nasal downpours.

Waiting for Morning

Nights were the hardest.

With each subsequent chemo treatment I found myself feeling weaker. The pain peaked over the weekends following the Neulasta shot. I battled long, sleepless nights. One night, at 3:30 a.m., I cried into my pillow. I moaned to Darrin, "I feel awful."

He stroked my back, "I'm so sorry. I wish I could take all the pain away."

I prayed, asking God to wake *everyone* and *anyone* to pray for me. I kept telling myself, "It will get better." But it didn't. I found no relief.

I felt so helpless, trapped inside my sick body.

Darrin eventually fell asleep. I didn't want to wake him with my tossing and turning, so I moved to the living room couch to try and get comfortable. I sat alone in the dark. I listened as the wind blew outside.

I listened to the kitchen clock tick. I waited for morning. And waited. Somehow in the light of day, my physical discomfort and emotional distress evened out, became manageable.

As the days moved along I still felt gross, but I stomached food again. Little signs gave me hope it would get better. My body ached deeply. First round had me worried something was amiss, but now I knew this came from the bone marrow regenerating itself.

I heard encouragement from sound-sleeping friends. "It's kind of strange. I normally sleep like a rock, but I woke up in the middle of the night with you on my mind, so I prayed for you." It happened with such frequency I began to value more profoundly the importance of prayer. Prayer was not reciting a laundry list of requests, penning a Christmas wish list to a cosmic vending machine. God intimately worked, hearing my cries, waking others to rally around me to help carry me through the dark nights that seemed to have no end.

Prior to my medical trial, I felt impatient whenever people shared prayer requests having to do with physical healing during Bible studies or over prayer chains. I would think to myself, *People are so full of pride. These prayer requests for health are a lame excuse. It's easier to pray for a neighbor's broken ankle than bring people into the reality of what is happening in their marriages or families, their finances, or their honest, deep struggles.*

After my diagnosis, I humbly confessed my own pride. While I still desired a deeper level of safety and honesty in these circles, I came to understand the vital role of prayer in physical trials. Prayer *mattered.* It made a difference in ways my finite mind could not grasp. When I couldn't pray for myself, it helped knowing God placed me on the heart and minds of others. He sustained me through their prayers. After those dark, painful nights, I wanted to be on any and every prayer chain, grateful anytime someone shared they had prayed for me.

Gracious Receiver

I got up earlier than normal one morning to fix lunch for Michael. He looked at me and said, "Mom, you don't need to make me lunches the next few days. I'm going to fast for you because I think it might help you during this round of chemo."

"Really, are you sure, Buddy? I thought they were serving pizza this week."

"Yeah, they are. But this is more important."

Michael chose to fast for me during the week he would be helping out in the school lunch line. Helping in the lunch line was a privilege reserved only for sixth graders. Helpers enjoyed access to pizza. Not cafeteria pizza, but *real* pizza delivered by an actual pizza chain. Pizza rated near the top as one of Michael's favorite foods.

Michael was forgoing pizza for me. I had no words.

One of the lessons I learned through the cancer journey was how to become a gracious receiver. I much preferred being on the giving side. It humbled me to be in a place to both need and receive help. Our family had been loved, prayed for, and helped in so many ways since the cancer journey began—particularly through our Crossroads Community Church family.

We could walk to our church. We probably lived the closest of all the families, but we consistently showed up late. People drove in on time from all around South Orange County. Up to an hour away, families would arrive from Orange, Placentia, Huntington Beach, and as far as Carlsbad. Crossroads, a church filled with people who genuinely loved God and each other, had the types of families I wanted to grow old with. Committed to excellence, the members displayed a wide array of talents and were warm, down to earth, and incredibly generous.

I think the entire church knew our garage code.

But as wonderful as our church friends and family were, I struggled.

I struggled with how *long* the treatment process took and how people continued to help us.

I struggled with not wanting to be a burden.

I struggled with comparing myself to others and thinking other women with breast cancer were back living life at 100 percent, so I shouldn't be a wimp. (Of course I didn't *know* any of these other women, but I'm sure they were out there.)

I struggled with thinking I should be farther along.

I struggled with not having the same capacity as before and being okay with not being able to *do*.

I would lie awake at night thinking about all my unwritten thank-you notes. I had to tell myself, *No one is lying awake right now waiting for a thank you from you, Viv. You are the only one thinking about this.* I grew tired of letting others help, always being a receiver. I realized this paralleled my inability to receive love and grace from God apart from performing and doing. I used to think God loved me more when I read my Bible, attended church, treated my family well, stayed busy in various Christian activities, and talked openly about Him with others. Instead the truth of being loved unconditionally began to change from head knowledge to knowing through experience. I was loved in whatever condition. God reformed my core through this time on some deep, deep levels.

Kitchen Camping

Tired of being in our bedroom staring at the ceiling, I began to migrate to new places to sleep. After another round of chemo, I found myself knocked out sleeping on the couch in the TV room. Around 2:30 a.m., the predictable pain peaked. I thought I'd done a good job of layering my pain and nausea meds, but I found myself unsuccessful. I wandered into the kitchen to get some water and then slid down to the floor.

Darrin came into the kitchen and looked at me sitting on the floor, leaning up against the cabinets by the kitchen sink.

I looked up. Assaulted by nausea, battling pain in my bones from my first vertebrate to my kneecaps, I didn't want to move. At all. "I'm not doing very well."

He sat down next to me on the kitchen floor. He said nothing. Leaning up against his arm was enough. After sitting for a long, long time on the kitchen floor in silence, Darrin asked, "Do you want to stay in the kitchen?"

I nodded.

He left the room. I heard the sound of a closet door open. I closed my eyes hoping it would quell the nausea. When I opened them again, Darrin stood at the doorway to the kitchen, arms full of sleeping bags and pillows. I watched as he set up camp for us. After I climbed into my sleeping bag, Darrin turned out the light. As I lay on the hard white tiles on kitchen floor in the dark next to Darrin, his broad chest breathing of deep sleep, I fell into a fitful sleep wondering, *How much more can I take?*

As the day streamed in through the kitchen windows, I knew the battle still raged on. I knew chemo had more to take from me and to teach me. But I also knew I'd make it.

Because I had Darrin.

Because my children pulled for me.

Because our church family tangibly loved us.

Because people prayed for me.

And all of that told me that no matter what chemo took from me, it had given me far more. Life, yes. But also blessings I would never had known—or allowed myself to accept—without what I struggled through.

behind the clouds

We look not at the things which are seen, but at the things which are not seen; for the things which are seen are temporal, but the things which are not seen are eternal.

2 Corinthians 4:18

The first weekend in June 2006, two-and-a-half years before my cancer journey, I participated in the Danskin Women's Triathlon in San Dimas, California. Leila thought it would be the perfect way to mark the milestone of turning forty. It's still a mystery why I agreed. We decided to take the team approach, so Leila swam, our friend, Joanna, biked, and I ran. Sally Edwards, the founder of the Danskin Triathalon, was in her seventies, and she participated every year in every race. And every time she crossed the starting line first and the finish line last so that someone else wouldn't have to come in last place.

Prior to training for this 5K, I had never jogged farther than a mile. Leila and I decided to start our training at Lake Mission Viejo— the perfect location. I could watch our kids while she practiced swimming laps in the lake; then we would switch, and she would watch the kids while I ran along the path. I stretched out on the sidewalk, using every stretch I could remember from my aerobics days when I used to work out. The kids played in the sand. In the distance Leila swam back and forth in the water.

When it was my turn, I set my watch so it could record my time, heart rate, and distance. I had a heart rate monitor strapped around my rib cage, which gave me a more official runner-look. Once I hit the start button, I took off. As I ran, my chest tightened. Then my legs began to burn. That's when it hit me . . .

Oh no. What have I gotten myself into? I hate *running.*

I kept going. Now my heartbeat pounded in my ears. My lungs joined my legs in a searing burn. My thoughts shifted.

I can't breathe.

I think I'm going to die right here on this path.

I hate running.

I hate Leila.

I cannot go any further.

Must. Stop. Now.

I stopped. I bent over with my hands on my knees, breathing hard through my mouth. I couldn't hear anything but the pounding of my heart. My face flushed. I looked at my watch.

One minute, thirteen seconds.

I had a long way to go.

But I kept training. Like every seasoned warrior, training provided skills and stamina to stay in the battle. I learned the discipline of showing up. Day to day the changes in my body and mind remained invisible, but over time transformation took place. Everyone begins a battle strong and fresh. Training, both mind and body, is what helped warriors persevere in order to see the battle to the end. Soon my run increased from one minute to ten minutes. Eventually I ran a 5K without hating running or Leila. Meanwhile, Leila and Joanna trained for their events.

The night before the race, we stayed at Joanna's house. We left before dawn the next morning. The race commenced with the swim leg. The race officials permitted the professional racers in the water first, right behind Sally. Then different waves of participants from the general public would join the race. They divided groups by age into different colors, so they'd enter the lake in staggered waves rather than all at once. The oldest participants would go first, giving them the most time to finish the race. Since we were on the older side, Leila started her swim early. We cheered her from the beach as her pink wave started off. We lost sight of her in the mess of arms and legs kicking up the murky water toward the buoy in the lake's center. The yellow wave followed. Then the orange.

We stood near the shore as the pink-wave racers emerged from the water. No Leila. Then the orange and yellow racers ran out of the lake, dripping, shaking the water out of their ears, racing to the bike segment. The professional racers now had nearly finished the bike race. Still no Leila. We began to feel mild concern when she finally appeared, full of smiles. We cheered and congratulated her as she took the race chip and handed it to Joanna.

Joanna had her new racing bike and all her gear ready. She donned gloves, a helmet, bike shorts, sunglasses, and the camel water backpack with long tube straw that connected from her back to her mouth for drinking ease—looking like a model from a cycling catalog. By now the first wave of racers had completed all three legs of the race and walked around the display tents with Danskin medals around their necks. We cheered for Jo as she disappeared down the road.

Leila and I drank water to stay hydrated and talked to pass the time. The sun rose higher into the sky. The number of bikers return- ing for the transition to the running leg diminished. We walked over to the ticker, which counted all the racers. Thousands had crossed the line. No sign of Jo. Our eyes scanned the roads looking for her. When the gap between racers grew even longer, we worried. Perhaps the bike broke down? Maybe the heat was too much and she fainted? We talked about whether to request a golf cart to go search for our friend. We waited a few more minutes, and then, in the distance, we saw her peddling. We couldn't contain our excitement and relief in seeing her cross the bike line.

Now the sun stood completely overhead, and I worried I would be the last person to finish. But Jo said, "Don't worry, Viv, just don't get behind Sally."

When Joanna dismounted her bike and handed the race chip to me, I took off running. Because of the heat I drank lots of water to stay hydrated. About a mile into the run I needed to use the restroom— the downside of hydration. I stopped to use the restroom, came out to resume my run, and there in *front* of me I saw . . . you guessed it . . . *Sally.*

She ran with some older ladies. I stepped it up a bit to pass them and then I hit this long stretch of hot, dry nothingness. I didn't have an iPod to blast motivating music. As a total novice runner, I wore aerobic shoes instead of running shoes. The shoes pinched my toes as my feet swelled from the heat. I was tired, hot, and all by myself. Sally jogged behind me with the other ladies. As far as my eyes could see, no one ran anywhere ahead of me. All I could do? Put one foot in front of the other. All I could hear? The *crunch, crunch, crunch* of my shoes against the gravel.

This described well where I found myself now in my cancer run.

The novelty of chemo had worn off and I had to persevere through a long stretch of nothingness. Life became putting one foot in front of the other, *crunch, crunch, crunch.* The end loomed nowhere in sight, and a lot of road still lay ahead.

Not long ago Kelly asked, "Which round of chemo did you find to be the worst?"

My reply? "All of them."

Behind the Clouds

I continued to walk Debbie's Course. At the top of the ultra-mega-steep hill boasted a pretty spectacular view of the Saddleback Mountains. As a mountain loving kind of girl, my perspective restored when I looked at the mountains.

One day as I walked the course, the clouds shrouded the Saddleback Mountains. I knew the mountains stood there, but if I were new to the area, I wouldn't know of their existence based on what I saw at the top of the hill. Looking at the clouds reminded me of the previous New Year's Eve. Dylan, Darrin's older brother, his wife, Lisa, and their three kids flew in from Kona to enjoy several days at Disneyland. Our family met up with them and we shared some laid-back time walking around Downtown Disney, eating dinner at the Rainforest Café, and taking pictures next to the big Christmas tree in the lobby of the Grand Hotel next to California Adventure. It had only been nine days since learning of my diagnosis, and we still reeled from the news. It was a gift to have time with them in the midst of life being turned upside down.

We decided to bring in the New Year by going to Dylan's hotel room, which faced the park, so we could see the typically incredible Disney fireworks show. Right before midnight, huge clouds rolled in. Soon it was foggy and cold enough to see our breath. We could hear the fireworks, and we saw a few flashes through the fog, but everything happened behind the cold clouds.

As I walked Debbie's Course, my mind and heart were struck by the truth that unseen things happened in my life because of cancer. God accomplished His purposes in ways I did not understand and could not see

It is so easy to lose perspective when we can't see how what we do matters. I remember struggling as a mom of young ones, thinking, *All I do all day is wipe counters and butts. Does it even matter?*

God reminded me again as I walked. Yes, what we do matters.

My life somehow fit into a bigger, intricately woven tapestry. The people we met, the places we lived, none of those things were accidents.

God would not waste my pain, struggles, or hardships. He would use them for His purposes.

But sometimes those purposes stood behind the clouds.

As I walked, I began to find rest in knowing God would wipe away the clouds one day and I would see the things He accomplished through—and because of—this particular trial. Perhaps on this side of heaven, but if not, I made peace with the thought that I most likely wouldn't fully understand everything until I embraced Him.

Taiko Drums

My friend, Kiersten, was born to run. She didn't even need to train for long-distance races. During the summer, our two families met on opening weekend for a matinee showing of the new Pirates of the Caribbean movie. The lights dimmed but no Kiersten. I leaned over to her husband, Casey. "Where is Kiersten?"

"Oh, she'll be here soon. She got up this morning to run in a half marathon down in San Diego." And sure enough, just as the movie started, in bounded Kierstin. Finished a half marathon before I even brushed my teeth. No big deal.

Kierstin shared that when she ran the Los Angeles Marathon, drummers beat on huge Japanese taiko drums at the finish line. "You could hear the drums about a mile out. They grew louder with each stride and motivated the runners," she told me.

Having already likened my cancer journey to a race, I pictured those taiko drums marking the finish line. Like a warrior returning from battle, invigorated and worn, I also imagined the taiko drums playing the sound of victory.

Darrin and I knew the routine by heart after five rounds of chemo. Following each treatment, my body had three weeks to repair before the next round. As we did our first time, each appointment we would stop by and pick up a Subway sandwich on our way to the doctor's office. When we arrived we would put the sandwiches in the little dorm-sized refrigerator to eat later for lunch. The nurses hooked up my port, checked my blood count, returned with smiley faces drawn on the lab result paper, and then administered the chemo cocktail. I sat in a different reclining chair for each infusion and sat next to different cancer patients each time. When we finished Darrin took me to get frozen yogurt to celebrate.

The final round of chemo landed on the Wednesday after school let out for the summer. I woke up feeling both excitement at the thought of finishing and dread knowing all too well the pain and discomfort that awaited me in the coming days. I applied the numbing cream on thick because I would have no need for it after the next day. Darrin, the Handsome Sherpa, carried my big bag across the parking lot.

We were the last two in the infusion room after the final round of chemo—all the other patients had finished and left. The nurses had tears in their eyes as they watched Darrin and me hug a long, long time, standing in the middle of the empty room. He held me strong, just like he did when we first received the diagnosis. I wept exhausted, grateful tears.

I had grown accustomed to seeing his head bald all these months. My family had grown used to seeing me bald, too. I only wore my scarves when I went out in public. My bald head, on this day, was covered by a black head covering.

I fumbled around in my purse and pulled out the small white box I had kept in my jewelry drawer for this very day. Darrin gently placed a silver necklace around my neck. When the Amazing Viv (a friend from church) first gave it to me, I decided to save it for the last day of chemo to wear as a medal.

We made it.

When we returned home, the Awesomes surprised me in the kitchen with flowers and balloons and banged madly on pots and pans—my own personal taiko drums. Gathering the flowers in my arms and sharing hugs all around, I felt like a warrior returning home from battle.

Waiting for the Final Bell

The days following the last round blurred by. I spent most of the time passed out on the couch in the TV room. I remembered back to when I first started chemo and called Karyn several times during the week to ask questions about all the different pills I needed to take. I couldn't keep straight which ones were for what. Now I rifled through the box full of meds with ease and counted on my fingers how many hours until the next dose. I filled out the meds chart dutifully, thankful that in three weeks I would no longer have to repeat the madness. The summer heat along with the hot flashes had me waking up drenched in sweat.

After several days, I finally took a shower—which wiped me out. Still very weak, I knew better days would come. I couldn't wait for the final bell to mark the end of the fight.

Jonathan returned home from a week-long camp in Northern California. Most of the families at our church attended Mount Hermon every year.

The day Jonathan returned he went straight to bed—and woke up with a high fever. The next day we received an e-mail that confirmed swine flu circulating among the high school group. So many kids got sick following camp that a camper created a Facebook group called "I Got Sick at Mount Hermon."

At my absolute lowest after six rounds of chemo, I could not get sick. Darrin disinfected the entire house. Julia caught the bug, followed by Michael. Darrin became sick. I miraculously escaped, except for a bad head cold.

As missionaries with Cru, we had a number of churches supporting us. We attended Oceanside Christian Fellowship while on staff at the UCLA campus. The prayer team there, led by Wanda, had e-mailed the previous month requesting specific prayer requests. The prayer team would focus on praying for our family during July. The request I sent Wanda was for a cone of protection as I finished my last round of chemo.

I am convinced the prayers of the OCF prayer team protected me from catching the flu.

Caught by Surprise

As my body continued to heal and bounce back, I found myself surprised by a flood of emotions. I fully expected to be on a total high coming off my last round of chemo—high-fiving everyone, happy and relieved. Instead I found myself sitting on my bed, bewildered.

What just happened to me? Who was the bald person with nearly invisible eyebrows looking back at me in the mirror?

Six months into treatment and my body still did not feel like my body. I would look at myself in the mirror, at the scars from the surgeries, and feel like Vivian inhabited someone else's body.

One book I read, written by a doctor who was a breast cancer survivor, captured what I felt. This doctor explained that she had treated cancer patients for years, but it took her own diagnosis for the irony to hit home—how so many start treatment much stronger than they end it. How having cancer is hard and traumatic, especially because of how debilitated patients feel during and after treatment.

Debilitated described well how I felt. I was physically and emotionally worn out. I gained the expected ten pounds from the chemo and steroids. I also experienced the hot flashes and mood swings resulting from chemical-induced menopause. *Chemopause* became one of many new words in my growing cancer vocabulary. I also experienced delayed emotional reactions.

When I used to run up the ultra-mega-steep hill, I kept my head down looking at the asphalt, hoping to avoid the parked cars and trash cans. I needed to muster every drop of physical energy to run up the hill. I'd made it through chemo the same way—one step to the next. But now?

That race finished. And without the focus of getting up the steep hill of chemo, I now started to assess and feel and react. And boy did I feel! One emotion after another. Anger at cancer and the way it ruined and took lives. Sadness because I missed the life I used to have and the path I walked before cancer. Confusion, asking myself over and over, *What happened?*

But as those emotions coursed through me, God did an amazing thing. He expanded my heart and helped me empathize with people who had difficulty trusting God. In the past I felt impatient when others shared their legitimate concerns:

If I choose to trust God and break up with my boyfriend who doesn't share my same commitment to God, will I end up alone?

God is calling me to serve Him overseas. Can I trust Him? Will He provide meaningful relationships? A spouse?

What if God's plan for my life doesn't include getting married and having kids?

Babies are left to die at the city dump in countries overseas, and my husband and I are unable to conceive. How can God allow this?

I gave God my whole life and chose to serve Him through vocational ministry, and now my own children have chosen to walk away from God. How does this happen?

For them, trusting God in the midst of the unknown, in the center of unanswered questions, of bewildering circumstances was difficult. Now I understood. Yes, it *is* hard to trust God when life doesn't make sense.

In the stew of those unexpected emotions, I returned to the truth that my anger, sadness, questions, doubt, and anything else I experienced didn't surprise or shock God. I'd spent a good portion of my life before cancer encouraging people to follow God fully—the most reasonable response in light of who He is. God is all knowing and all powerful. He is all loving. He is just, holy, faithful, and kind. He is good. And regardless of my feelings, He remains unchanging. Battling cancer enlarged my heart to wrestle with God over the harder questions I normally brushed over.

Now, in the face of all I'd endured, I no longer needed to pretend things were okay when they weren't. Because God understood. He stood by me in the midst of what didn't feel good. Rather than pull away from God in the dark times, I sought to move *toward* Him in the raw and real. And most amazing of all . . .

He welcomed my questions, my confusion, my anger, my pain.

He welcomed all of me.

Gotta Share the Moment

One morning a few weeks later, after I washed my face, I saw a brand new layer of *eyebrows* growing! I ran out to the backyard to share the moment with Darrin. He came inside and confirmed, yes, indeed, new eyebrows had grown in!

I pointed out the new sprouts to Julia the next day and she said, "Wow, Mom! Now I can't even count how many eyebrows you have." Just the week before Julia gave me the eyebrow hair tally: eleven hairs on the right brow, fourteen on the left.

My head also had light peach fuzz growing. It felt like newborn baby hair. Darrin stopped shaving his head, and his hair growth looked like a Chia Pet. Amazing growth.

Seeing signs of new growth brought tremendous encouragement.

Another Detour

I began to experience pain in my right arm and loss of range of motion. I woke up with increased swelling in my arm. After I called the doctors' offices I sat, waiting, concern growing. Everything pointed to symptoms of lymphedema, a swelling in the interstitial spaces in our bodies caused by the inability of the lymphatic system to carry away accumulated fluid.

Basically, I had excess fluid and swelling in my arm because I had all my lymph nodes under my arm removed. The fluid couldn't drain on its own and needed to be moved manually to working lymph nodes. Unlike the brain, where it can actually learn to rewire after trauma, the lymphatic system doesn't naturally redirect the fluid. I knew I would feel varying levels of awful going into chemo so I mentally prepared for when the time came. But this new challenge caught me off guard. I knew something wasn't right but I didn't know what. All I wanted to do was sit in a pile and shut out the world and bawl.

So I did.

I struggled to wrestle my compression sleeve onto my arm—a super uncomfortable, extra-thick support hose thing that covered my entire arm. The sleeve helped redirect the lymphatic fluid. I'd known I would need to wear my compression sleeve and a gauntlet on my hand during airplane rides and whenever the elevation was above 3,500 feet, but I had hoped to be in the 80 percent category of women

CaringBridge

God is always at work, and sometimes I don't take the time to pause and watch for Him. I've been thinking about God sightings from the last week or so, and I wanted to share a couple.

The first one was on the day of my surgery last week. At the surgery center I laid in my bed waiting for the doctor. Four, maybe five beds, all separated by those hospital curtains, lined up against the wall and mine was the one on the end. The nurse in charge of me came bounding in through the curtain full of enthusiasm and spunk—she reminded me of Tigger from *Winnie the Pooh*. I noticed on her name tag a pink breast cancer sticker. She looked at me and said, "I am a breast cancer survivor, and I want you to know that I was lying in who didn't deal with lymphedema. My lymphedema specialist, Gina, had given me exercises for manual lymph drainage and lymphedema exercises. I knew I should start them, but discouragement weighed so heavy on me that I found myself digging in my heels, resisting what I knew would be good.

I was so tired of being a patient.

I was so in need of learning to *be* patient.

I planned to make the last weeks before radiation and the start of a new school year a carefree off-treatment break. I wanted to enjoy a few weeks of feeling good. I wanted normal—some days strung together without doctors' offices and waiting rooms. But lymphedema thwarted my plans—an unwanted detour in a year that had become one gigantic detour.

Axillary Web Syndrome

As if the fluid build-up wasn't bad enough, I had increasing difficulty straightening out my arm. My range of motion became even more limited.

As soon as my doctor saw me she knew exactly what I battled—axillary web syndrome, also known as cording. She also confirmed I also had

the exact same bed in this exact same slot two years ago. I had the same procedure with the same surgeon and anesthesiologist and I picked them because they are the best. I know because I am a nurse and work with all the doctors. You are in great hands." I went in to surgery so encouraged and at peace. Just the right person at just the right time. God has been so faithful to provide what I've needed each step of the way.

The other God sighting was seeing how He continues to encourage and remind me of His love through His people. This whole cancer journey has taken soooooooo long. I am impatient. I am creeping along at a snail's pace and life—normal life—continues on at a hundred miles a minute. Sometimes I feel like yesterday's news, and I struggle with feeling forgotten. But as I look back even on these last few weeks, especially these last few days, I am struck with God's amazing timing.

Gifts and messages of love from His people . . .

- Flowers on my doorstep.
- A phone call from someone saying, "I'm bringing dinner tonight."
- A bookmark received today, discovered by the sender, who had meant to send it three years ago! The message on the bookmark: "Keep Pushing On" and Philippians 4:13: "I can do all things in Him who strengthens me."
- Another card and gift arrived—originally given to Leila to pass along to me back in May, but got lost in a pile. It turned up again at just the right time. Filled with written words I needed to hear, "You're gonna make it Viv; the Lord is your strength. Continue to take care and allow others and God to shower you with love."

lymphedema. She pointed out the cords sticking out right where my arm bent. They looked like extra tendons, like thick twine under the skin. I felt relieved to learn I didn't imagine my pain and discomfort. What a comfort to be understood and validated.

She mentioned most surgeons did not know about AWS, but it was common with breast cancer patients who had lymph nodes removed. As a breast cancer survivor herself, diagnosing and treating lymphedema landed high on her priority list. When I wore my compression sleeve during an airplane ride months before it had slipped on easily. Now it hurt to slip on and take off.

I learned radiation could also cause more cording, so I needed to continue physical therapy appointments throughout radiation treatment.

Sigh.

Chemo had seemed impossible to get through at the time, so I figured anything after it would be easy. I anticipated being able to run down hill for the duration of treatment where I wouldn't need to exert as much emotional or physical energy. But then I remembered that similar to hiking or running, going downhill can hurt too. It has its own challenges and still requires focus.

This cancer marathon still loomed before me.

Darrin mentioned marathon runners dealt with new pains toward the end of the race. New pains. On top of the pains they already battled.

I could relate.

Somehow I'd pictured this stage with me waving at the crowds, high steppin' it, wearing a big ol' smile, more waving. Now . . .

At best I would crawl over the finish line. Maybe roll.

Timely words. God's provision and reminders of His presence. His perfect timing. His people prompted. Fills my heart with hope and encouragement. Fills my eyes with tears.

Watch for God. He is always at work. Thanks for your continued prayers and encouragement. Thanks for being a part of my God sightings because I see Him when I see you.

I participated in a race I didn't train for.

I battled though I didn't enlist.

Cancer had stretched and challenged me on every level.

Cancer made for the hardest year of my life.

Surely things couldn't get worse.

8
the little things

You know when I sit down and when I rise up; You understand my thought from afar. You scrutinize my path and my lying down, and are intimately acquainted with all my ways.

Psalm 139:2–3

The day I drove to the radiation oncologist office for a CT scan, southern California experienced heat-wave temperatures. High nineties and desert dry. Earlier that day Katherine, Julia's friend, blurted out in the car, "It was like 435 degrees yesterday!"

Yup, that's exactly what it felt like.

As I pulled into the full parking lot and circled around, the perfect shaded parking spot waited for me. A little gift from heaven.

Inside, as I lay down for the CT scan and passed through the tube, listening to the hum and clicks of the machine, I sensed God being right with me. As if He said, "I know where you are, Viv, and how you are feeling. I know when you show up to appointments and which parking spots you like. I'm right here with you as you move through this cold machine. I am here. I am near."

I asked to see the big radiation machines before I left. They were in two different rooms. One machine would be used for the majority of the radiation treatments, the zaps alternating between the scar area and the entire chest area. I'd spend the last week of treatment under the other machine, targeting just the scar area—an extra concentrated boost to kill off any lingering cancer cells. Apparently the most commonplace spot for cancer to return is in the scar tissue. The machines looked high-tech and futuristic.

I remembered seeing artistic black and white photos in my doctor's office of a bald woman with nickel-size tattoos on her sternum. To my surprise, the radiation tech informed me the tattoos I would receive would be smaller than most of my moles. Used to accurately line up the radiation machines, the tattoos would mark off the field for the treatment. In a matter of minutes, after being lined up under the radiation machine, the tech dotted me. Three clear stickers covered the three tiny blue dots stuck across my chest and stomach. The waterproof stickers needed to stay in place until the following week when the radiation tech would tattoo the little blue dots permanently. I would not be able to receive radiation treatment in the same area again because of the radiation's potency.

I would face a total of thirty-three sessions of radiation therapy. Thirty-three didn't sound so bad. Six and half weeks sounded overwhelming, but not thirty-three sessions, so Julia and I decided to use our Origami paper we bought in Japan the previous summer to make a paper chain—one link for each session of radiation. She looked forward to cutting a link off the chain after each treatment as a countdown.

Wolverine

I lost count of how many medical appointments I experienced, and yet I faced more. Once again I sat in a waiting room, waiting for a follow-up appointment. I learned to knit scarves while waiting. This time I connected with two fellow breast cancer comrades further down the recovery road than me. I had hair growing back on my head—for which I thanked God—but also Wolverine sideburns growing on my face—which horrified me! These kind ladies assured me Wolverine sideburns were normal, and that the new facial hair wouldn't be permanent.

What a relief to know that my visions of joining the circus as the bearded lady wouldn't come true.

Radiation

I asked Darrin to join me for the first and last radiation appointments. As he drove me to that first appointment, he asked, "How do you feel going into radiation?"

I teared up. "I just want to be done. I'm weary and tired and there is no way to hurry this process. I'm grateful for the technology, but this whole thing has just gone on for so long."

I wouldn't begin my radiation treatments feeling 100 percent. The night before my first appointment, Julia and I painted our nails. As I removed my nail polish, I noticed again my gray-colored nails and the deep chemo ridges. My body ached, and it took a while for the soreness to go away whenever I sat for an extended amount of time. I wore the compression sleeve daily to help with the lymphedema.

Paper Chain and Parking Angels

After the eighth treatment the radiation countdown paper chain no longer touched the floor. I struggled with fatigue, but that battle had more to do with adjusting to the back-to-school schedule and shuttling three kids to three schools than the radiation.

I had a rough weekend. Short with the kids, edgy, irritable, moody, grumpy. I barked orders, expressed my disapproval indirectly. It wasn't so much what I was saying, but *how* I was saying it.

"Seriously! You have got to start your homework! Quit playing around!"

"Why am I dumping out all this food? Why are you so opposed to eating leftovers? This is so wasteful! You should be grateful we even have food!"

"This room is a disaster! I can't even see the floor. How can you live this way?"

"Why did you wait until the last moment to hand me this packet of forms to fill out?"

I could have picked helpful words and not raised my voice.

I could have used their mistakes and bad attitudes as teaching moments.

I could have apologized for my nasty tone.

But I didn't.

My moodiness settled over our home, creating an icy winter like the land of Narnia from C. S. Lewis's classic, *The Lion, the Witch, and the Wardrobe*. Always winter and never Christmas. I resembled the evil white witch—no longer the wife or mom I wanted to be.

Monday rolled around, and I had to drive to the dungeon for another five consecutive days of radiation treatments. The actual zapping happened relatively quickly—the length about three rounds of singing the "Happy Birthday" song—but the driving, parking, checking in, waiting, changing into my medical gown, zapping, and changing clothes again took nearly an hour.

As I turned in, preparing to circle around and around, God provided perfect parking under the shade tree. Perfect parking continued throughout the day. I mean, seriously, the closest spot right next to the handicap one at the mall, the closest spot at Target, shade at the grocery store, no circling around, no vulture parking, just seamless perfect parking. Everywhere I drove the parking angel saved me a spot during the busiest time of day. I sat in the car with my arms over the steering wheel and looked up to the sky, "I *so* don't deserve this, God. You saw how I acted over the weekend."

He spoke to my heart, "Viv, I'm fond of you. My love and grace and favor aren't based on what you do."

Grace is unmerited favor—a lesson I needed to learn and relearn. I had grown up thinking if my good outweighed my bad, at the end of my life, I would be granted access to heaven, basing God's acceptance of me solely on my performance. Once I started reading the Bible, I finally understood the meaning of grace and that access to heaven didn't depend on being a "good person."

"For by *grace* you have been saved through faith; and that not of yourselves, it is the gift of God; not as a result of works, so that no one may boast" (Ephesians 2:8–9, emphasis mine).

God's favor didn't depend on how I performed. Even my "good works" were often tainted by impure motives. I used to think of myself as a nice person, a helpful wife. But later God's Spirit pointed out my motive for being nice didn't always stem from caring about Darrin, but from trying to manipulate and control his emotions. I tried to head off his anger or disappointment through trying to anticipate his wants and needs. Rather than seek for his good and love my husband well, my thoughtful actions derived from a selfish need to control. Right behavior could originate from a place of selfishness. What relief to learn God's unmerited favor came with no strings attached. Lessons on God's unconditional love and grace continued to shift me from what I thought I knew to what I finally understood about grace.

Race for the Cure

We decided to participate in the Susan G. Komen Race for the Cure as a family. After signing up, I looked through all the fun gear on the display tables. I noticed a pink survivor hat and then it hit me: I was a surVIVor! My name sat smack-dab in the middle of that powerful word! I had been reluctant to refer to myself as a survivor because I still walked through treatment. Technically I still fell under breast cancer *patient*. But after thinking about it I decided that after all I walked through in the past nine months, I qualified as a survivor! So I happily picked up a surVIVor hat for the race!

That switch in thinking changed me.

I found new strength and renewed hope.

The Race for the Cure event both encouraged and sobered me. I thought the boys would complain about waking up early on the one morning they could sleep in and wearing pink T-shirts, but they had great attitudes. Julia wore a pink T-shirt proclaiming on front "In my lifetime," conveying the hope that a cure for cancer would be found within her lifetime.

They scheduled a special tribute for breast cancer survivors before the race. Volunteers passed out pink roses to each of us, and different speakers shared about their own cancer journeys. At the end, a woman stood on the steps in front of the sea of pink and sang the Celine Dion song "Because You Loved Me." During the song, I lost it. Darrin held me as I stood in the survivor section sobbing, he on the other side of the race tape that divided us. All the memories from the past year tumbled through my mind. I cried tears of gratefulness, exhaustion, and grief.

The race itself (actually, a walk) was low-key but packed. People walked their dogs; kids rode along on their scooters; groups of people wore funny costumes and custom-made T-shirts; and a marching band marched passed us (did I mention it was a *slow* walk?). Groups of people stood on the sidelines, looking for women wearing the hot pink survivor T-shirts. They cheered as each survivor passed by. Pinned on the backs of many participants were pink papers that read, "In celebration of" and "In memory of." Posters of memorialized women lined the course. Many had passed away during the previous calendar year. Along the course, different bands played live music, which helped the race feel festive and upbeat.

At the end of the race a group of taiko drummers played.

We took a family picture under the finish line sign and used it for our Christmas card photo a few months later. It captured what our year had been like, the battle we had faced and the fact we had finished it . . .

Together.

Tents

When my younger sister, Claire, and I were probably about eight and eleven years old, we had the wonderful idea of setting up the blue, two-man tent in our backyard, like a makeshift playhouse—all this during summertime when violent thunderstorms appeared out of nowhere in Boulder. We filled the tent with our stuffed animals, pillows, and Oreos. I remember needing to unzip the front flap regularly because it got stuffy inside the tent.

Content, we had our own special space; we set up our little world just the way we wanted. We came up with an elaborate, make-believe kingdom where our stuffed animals played characters in an important story line and we, as the adults, called the shots.

One day I heard thunder so loud the ground shook followed by winds so strong the rain blew sideways. The poles of the tent bent. We screamed at the top of our lungs as the thunder continued and then cried big tears that rivaled the big raindrops. We held each other as we prepared to *die . . . outside . . .* in our supposedly safe tent.

And then we heard the familiar voice of our sweet grandma who stood barely four-foot-nine. She stood outside the tent, her hair blowing and the umbrella she held flipping inside-out from the wind. We managed to untangle our arms to unzip the front flap.

She said to us in Chinese, "It's really stormy out here. You should go inside."

So, we climbed out of the tent and walked the fifteen feet to our back door and into our warm, safe house. We left the flattened blue tent with our soggy animals and Oreos outside.

As I looked back on our adventure that day, I realized my body felt much like the tent. I walked through life assuming I could set up my little world mostly the way I wanted. I had my plans and, on a certain level, thought I would be the one to call the shots. But just like the blue tent bent by the winds, my body showed its vulnerabilities, how prone it was to falling apart.

Cancer, like the storm, revealed my helplessness.

My body did not obey my mind. Every morning I felt robbed. My eyes would open, and I would lift my arms up and look at my hands. My fingers would be slightly bent in a receive-a-blessing position like when our pastor, Pastor Kevin, would pray a blessing at the end of our weekly church service.

I tried with all my might to close my fist.

No go.

What I thought a function as natural as blinking and breathing, the ability to open and close my hands, now disappeared. Taken from me. I wondered if people who struggled with arthritis woke in the same pain. The doctors told me my lack of estrogen opened my hands. The chemo sent me early and abruptly into menopause. Instead of my body having several years to get used to not having this lovely hormone, I experienced a crash-course adjustment. After my body warmed up, I would regain the ability to close my fist, but things like getting out of my car or getting off the floor after playing a board game with the kids left me stiff and achy. I would mumble out loud, but to myself, as I used furniture to help me move from place to place, *Old lady, old lady, old lady.*

Most of the people I interacted with in different waiting rooms were older than me. Often much, much older. Even the folks who brought the patients to the appointments were older. As I sat waiting, I watched. My world now included women and men confined to wheelchairs, bodies bent over, white hair, faces lined with years of joy and sorrow. I looked into their eyes and realized anew that the truest part of a person wasn't fully represented in the physical body. The tents we inhabit are temporal: our bodies age, and ache, and break down. But there is more to us than just a physical body.

"Therefore we do not lose heart. Though outwardly we are wasting away, yet inwardly we are being renewed day by day. For our light and momentary troubles are achieving for us an eternal glory that far outweighs them all. So we fix our eyes not on what is seen, but on what is unseen, since what is seen is temporary, but what is unseen is eternal. For we know that if the earthly tent we live in is destroyed, we have a building from God, an eternal house in heaven, not built by human hands. Meanwhile we groan, longing to be clothed instead with our heavenly dwelling" (2 Corinthians 4:16–5:2 NIV).

These new aches and pains are a part of the aging process. God knows the exact day I will be rid of this fallen, earthly tent, the day I will walk those fifteen feet across the lawn into heaven. No more storms, no more pain.

Truly safe and warm at last.

Finish Line

Banana bread baked in the oven, and the delicious smell filled the house. I knew the recipe by heart. My Bible study leader from college, Shelley, shared it with me all those years ago, and I thought of her every time I baked it. Marvelous in every way, Shelley—a gifted teacher, singer, baker, creative genius—helped lead the Cru staff team when I studied at the University of Colorado. She did everything with excellence.

Twenty years ago Shelley took time to sit down with me and challenge me to join the staff of Cru, and to this day, I still felt grateful. She poured her life into mine, and I try to do the same in the lives of other women.

Hebrews 13:7 says, "Remember those who led you, who spoke the word of God to you; and considering the result of their conduct, imitate their faith." Next to this verse in my Bible I wrote the names of the women who mentored and trained me: Irene, Jeni, Shelley, Taryn, Charmaine, and Prisca. I lost contact with one, but all the rest I called not only mentors, but also close friends. God used each of these women at pivotal times in my life. My faith developed, in large part, because of their investment in my spiritual life.

As I took the banana bread out of the oven, I realized how God used so many friends, family, and even strangers during my battle with cancer to bless me. I stood grounded in my faith because of the prayers, love, gifts, help, encouragement, and friendship of those who came alongside me. Words could not do justice to, or capture the depth of, the gratitude I felt inside.

During the last part of my run in the Danskin Triathlon, after not seeing anyone during the long stretch of hot gravel, I finally saw a man in his seventies walking toward me on the opposite side of the road. He smiled and waved at me, and then pointed behind him and said, "It gets better up ahead!"

I nodded, smiled, and waved back, wondering what he meant.

And then the road curved around to a lush, tree- and grass-filled park.

Shade. Music. People taking down their exhibits (remember we were toward the end, just a little before Sally). Women walking their bikes back to their cars, their medals hanging around their necks. Smiling faces.

And then I saw Michael and Julia jumping up and down, waving wildly. I couldn't hold back the tears. My little Asian nose has no bridge so my sunglasses rested on my checks, and my tears filled up my glasses like a submarine submerging. I kept lifting up my sunglasses to let out the tears so I could see ahead. Then, further down, I spied Darrin and Jonathan. More tears.

The finish line came into my line of sight. Excitement sent my heart pumping harder and a new rush of energy washed over me. Leila and Joanna jumped in alongside me, and we held hands and ran across the finish line together!

Now, the finish line for active treatment was only days away. Once again, excitement pumped my heart. I heard taiko drums in my mind. I pictured holding hands and crossing the finish line with Darrin, the kids, the Awesome Threesome—with all those who had prayed for and supported me in hundreds and thousands of ways.

We *would* finish the race.

Together.

9

room for another

I will give you the treasures of darkness, and hidden wealth of secret places, so that you my know that it is I, the LORD, the God of Israel, who calls you by name.

Isaiah 45:3

During the last week of radiation treatment I often fell asleep with tears rolling out of my eyes into my ears. The house would finally quiet and my heart would finally quiet . . . and then the tears would begin their silent descent from my eyes into my ears. Not the sobbing kind of tears, just quiet tears.

The end of active treatment meant Julia had to step onto a dining room chair to cut the remaining paper links. The technicians moved me to the room next door, which held the other zapping machine for boosts targeted to the scar area. The skin on my chest raged an angry red, like a horrible sunburn. My T-shirts constantly smelled of aloe vera gel.

Only four more radiation treatments left.

The tears I cried meant many things. Relief, gratefulness, grief, joy, exhaustion, pity, pride, anger, appreciation, confusion, disbelief, sadness, and happiness all rolled together. Even I, someone who loves words, could not adequately describe how I felt. Words seemed too small. Words could not capture the myriad feelings.

Only tears.

Last Day

Darrin took a ministry trip to Seattle. He got up at four a.m. so he could make it back in time for my last radiation appointment. Unfortunately, his plane was delayed in San Francisco. The Awesome Threesome took pictures with me in the waiting room, and then I went back and changed into the all-too-familiar hospital gown. The techs were full of smiles as they lined me up and then shut the two, five-inch-thick steel doors behind them for the last time.

I couldn't hold back the tears, so just let them roll out of my eyes.

As soon as I returned to the dressing room, I called Darrin and left him a voice mail, my voice choking out the words: "Darrin. It's Viv. We did it! We're done!"

I threw on my clothes and walked out to the waiting room. The Awesomes stood and clapped and wept with me. We hugged and took pictures. Kelly brought out a beautiful lei. Then they whisked me off to a surprise lunch at a sushi restaurant.

At the restaurant, Faye, Margaret, Lucy, Melissa, Missy, the Amazing Viv, Joanne, and Brent joined us. More tears. More hugs. The Amazing Viv tied pink helium balloons to mini sparkling apple cider bottles with personalized labels. She painted a big banner:

CONGRATULATIONS!

YOU DID IT!

WE ARE SO PROUD OF YOU.

Totally amazing.

We gathered around the table when Darrin finally arrived, beautiful roses in hand. His eyes looked tired from the early morning flight, his face weary and worn out from the battle.

But he wore a smile as he hugged me and whispered in my ear, "You did it. I'm so proud of you."

I pulled away and looked into his eyes with tears in my own. *"We* did it."

We ate delicious food, and then most everyone returned to work. The Amazing Viv had the idea for a balloon release to celebrate letting go this season of battling cancer. So the Awesomes, Melissa, the Amazing Viv, and I gathered the balloons and walked outside. Each of them held a pink balloon, and I grasped a white one. I shared some words of gratitude to God and to them.

"This has been *by far* the hardest year of my life. I had no way of knowing what life would look like after getting my diagnosis. So many times I didn't think I would make it to the end of cancer treatment. Now, looking back, I realize the integral part each of you played in helping carry my family and me all these months."

Glancing around the circle with the warmth of the sun on my face, the fragrance of the lei around my neck, heart bursting with gratitude, my voice quivered.

"My heart is thankful heart to God in large part due to the ways each of you loved me. I love you all so much. I don't think I will ever find enough ways to express my appreciation for you and for all you've done. We have battled together each step of the way. And God has been kind to me."

Lifting my balloon higher into the air I continued, "Today marks the end of active treatment, so with the release of these balloons, we say good-bye to this cancer chapter. By letting go, our hands are symbolically open to the future and whatever else God brings."

We released the balloons together, watching as they disappeared into the clear, blue California sky. The music piping into the mall area made the moment feel like a music video, or the end of a Korean soap opera.

We laughed through the tears, but also thought the music fit the moment perfectly.

On December 22, 2008, I received the phone call: "You have cancer."

Exactly ten months later—after three surgeries, six rounds of chemo, thirty-two physical therapy sessions, thirty-three radiation treatments, and countless doctors' appointments, pills, blood work, and scans, the active treatment was *done*!

I was a full-on surVIVor!

After the Storm

I found myself *extremely* tired. The doctors explained I would continue to feel fatigue for the first two weeks following radiation as my body continued to heal and repair. Earlier I asked how X-rays differed from the radiation. The tech explained, "When you deal with X-rays the voltage is in the thousands, with radiation, it's in the millions."

I felt shell-shocked, too, with treatment coming to an abrupt end.

The best metaphor I found to describe what I felt: life following a hurricane. The first hurricane I experienced (they call those storms *typhoons* in Hong Kong) was Typhoon Ellen in 1983.

The news reports on the radio spoken by a British newscaster declared Typhoon Ellen the worst typhoon in a hundred years. Somehow the British accent added to the severity. My sister, Claire, and I stood watching outside on our little balcony, clearly new to the typhoon scene. Mouths open, we marveled at the downpour . . . or more like side-pour of rain. Sheets of rain. Blinding rain. Nothing remotely close to anything we experienced in Colorado. Our umbrellas and raincoats proved useless, and we returned inside completely drenched.

We lived on the top floor of a four-floor flat (a.k.a. large apartment) in Kowloon. The rooftop area above us was a large, walled, tiled expanse. When we first moved in we would run up to the roof to watch the jumbo jets flying overhead with their wheels down ready to land. We had never seen airplanes fly so close. We thought we could hit one with our sandals. Water now covered the roof area. The excess water flooded out the doorway. When we opened our front door, the staircase outside looked like a waterslide. The rushing, swirling waterfall worked itself from the flooded roof down to the ground floor. The sound of the storm was so loud we had to yell to hear each other.

The next morning fallen trees covered our entire street. Officials cancelled school for several days. The streets were uncommonly quiet. People emerged from their homes to assess the damage. A mixture of relief and anxiety filled the air. Life felt awkward and uncomfortable.

Life after cancer treatment felt like that as well, but on the inside. For ten months I felt like I grabbed hold of a palm tree in the middle of a hurricane—one not forecasted that appeared out of nowhere. My nails dug deep into the tree trunk and I held on. Now the storm passed. Life felt uncommonly quiet, awkward and uncomfortable. Each day held so many mixed feelings: grateful to be alive, yet stunned and tired. Most days I tried to regain my bearings and assess the damage.

The Story of Max

Life continued to feel wobbly as our family climbed out from the rubble of cancer treatment. Darrin noticed we began to all withdraw emotionally. We needed to figure out and make sense of the madness we had walked through. But as we journeyed along, we seemed to drift apart, lost in our own worlds, as we sorted through the storm's aftermath.

Darrin resumed his demanding travel schedule. During one trip to Boston, I received a text as he sat waiting to return home. One of the men in his Tuesday night men's Bible study had a girlfriend who needed to find a home for her dog. The texts flew back and forth between us. Darrin ended up calling Claudia, the owner, and she told him about the dog.

Darrin texted: His name is Max.

Darrin boarded the flight. While he was in flight, I decided to call Claudia myself to get more background about the dog. She e-mailed a picture of Max and a YouTube link. I learned he came from a rescue shelter in Los Angeles. He was six months old when someone rescued him out of an abandoned car lot surrounded by animal carcasses.

Max was a fighter. He survived parvo, a highly contagious and dangerous virus. Housebroken, almost three years old, he had never bitten anyone, and he needed a big yard. After a couple years with a family, Max ended up living in an apartment with Claudia, Claudia's teenage daughter, and their golden retriever, Sunshine.

Apparently the apartment complex brimmed over with small dogs that liked to go after Max. The week before we talked with Claudia, her apartment association had given her an ultimatum because of Max's barking. If she didn't get rid of the dog, they would be evicted. They had until Friday.

Today was Thursday.

After dinner I gathered the kids around the dining room table. I showed the Youtube video of Max, and then explained his situation. Julia could not contain her excitement. She looked like she would float off her chair at the possibility of having a dog.

Swinging her legs excitedly under her chair, unable to wipe the smile from her face, she kept repeating, "Oh, my goodness. Really? Am I dreaming? Is this for real?"

Jonathan put his head down on the table in his arms. "I don't want any more responsibility." He was in the throes of the crazy, insane junior year of high school.

Michael, eyes bright, beamed from ear to ear.

Here's the amazing part of all this. Just three weeks earlier, Darrin and I had been out of town at a wedding. As we drove around and talked, out of the blue he asked me, "You ever think about us getting a dog?"

"Oh, I'd love to get a dog. What kind would you want if we could have one?"

"I like German shepherds. What about you?"

"I'd want a yellow lab."

We talked about how we would probably want to rescue a dog from a shelter and not buy one from a pet store.

Max was a mix—half German shepherd and half yellow lab. The name Max? Well, it happened to be Michael's favorite name growing up. He named everything Max. His screen name on all his computer games? Max. He even asked me around age five, "Mommy, why didn't you name me Max?"

With all these little details coming together, I couldn't help but wonder, *Lord, should we go for it?*

Darrin arrived at LAX, and we talked about Max as he drove home. After we finished our call, I called Claudia at 10:30 p.m. We had decided to take Max for a trial week to see how he liked our family.

Late Friday afternoon Max arrived with Sunshine, Claudia, her daughter, and all his stuff. We decided to have Sunshine stay with Max overnight to help ease the transition. Max and Sunshine went crazy running around in the backyard. He instantly took to Julia. Darrin arrived home and played with Max in the yard. I looked over at Claudia's daughter and asked her how she felt having to give Max away. She answered, "I'm okay." I could tell she was not.

"Do you believe in God?"

She nodded, and I explained the backdrop of the story. She smiled as she realized how God had worked behind the scenes. Max fit so perfectly with all we had talked about even before we knew he would end up with us.

Our week with Max flew by. It seemed like we had always had him. At the end of the week when we decided he would stay, Julia and I went to the pet store and bought him a new collar and a tag with his new last name and address.

Claudia shared later how, when they left Max at our house and got into their car, she and her daughter both cried all the way home. They loved Max, but they found comfort knowing Max had a big backyard now and a family that would love and care for him. When Claudia first received the letter threatening eviction she put calls into the local dog shelters. All of them were full. At one point she thought she would have to put Max down. She prayed for a home for Max. God answered her prayer. She felt thankful, and we felt thankful, too.

Claudia offered to come over and watch Max when we needed to go out of town for conferences. Much of our ministry work with staff and college students involved being away from home for weekends at retreats and conferences. Claudia's offer was a huge answer to a big concern. It had been the main reason why we had not pursued a dog earlier.

Max, jumpy and skittish around new people, had no problem being around kids. Loud noises scared him. Whenever we clipped our nails he would leave the room shaking. His caramel fur felt like velvet. He had the softest coat of fur I had ever felt on a grown dog. Every morning I would greet him, scratching his soft ears. "Max, you are God's gift to us. I am thankful for you every day." His tail wagged as he followed me to the kitchen and waited for the rest of the family to wake.

I loved how everything transpired. We weren't looking, and the dog came to us. Left to ourselves, we didn't have the energy and would not have researched to figure out how or where to rescue a dog. And even if we had gone to a shelter, we realized we would not have picked an initially timid dog like Max. But we had learned through cancer to be comfortable with the unexpected. Max fit our family.

As our family settled into life with Max, we realized God used the dog to bring us back together. He had a unique relationship with each one of us, and we all reconnected over our new family member. He gave us a new focus as we helped him transition to his new home. Max brought laughter back into our home, especially when Max would hear the doorbell on a TV show and run toward and bark at the front door.

We thought we rescued Max.

As it turned out, he rescued us.

10

the great celebration

*Enter His gates with thanksgiving, and His courts with praise.
Give thanks to Him, bless His name. For the LORD is good;
His lovingkindness is everlasting, and His faithfulness to all
generations.*

Psalm 100:4–5

The weeks following the end of active treatment I concentrated on the themes of gratitude and food. Cancer treatments ended as we entered the Thanksgiving season, my favorite holiday. We hosted Thanksgiving at our home as in the previous eleven years, since we moved into the house.

The kids continued the tradition with a simplified version of the annual Thanksgiving play. In years past, Kelly's kids, Matt and Anna, and the boys would plan for months writing a script which, at different points, included time travel, a smoke machine, huge refrigerator boxes, and scene changes. During those scene changes, Jaron, Leila's oldest son, would break dance; the younger kids performed stand-up knock-knock jokes or demonstrated a fancy light saber fight. One year Julia wore her pink princess dress and walked in front of the young actors while holding her huge stuffed Donkey from the movie *Shrek*. She stole the show.

Thanksgiving—a time when the house bustled with family and friends. Just the way I liked it.

Each year, I placed five popcorn kernels at each table setting. They symbolized the first Thanksgiving celebration, when the pilgrims rationed food because of a particularly harsh winter and the subsequent famine. During dinner, each person would take a turn and share five things they were thankful for, place the kernels into the green gourd votive, and pass it to the next person—one of my favorite Thanksgiving traditions.

Years back I asked the kids to list five things they were thankful for in a Thanksgiving Journal. Before they could write, I wrote down what they said. Soon the pages filled with large letters, with mixed up *b*s and *d*s, words sounded out and misspelled. I loved flipping through the journals year after year and reflecting on my children's growth and what stood out to them over the previous year. The kids usually needed a little prodding to figure out their five, so I asked Michael when I picked him up from school, "Hey, so it's Thanksgiving tomorrow. What are you thankful for this year?"

He didn't hesitate. "I'm thankful you're alive, Mom."

His answer shot through me and caught me off guard. I swallowed hard, thankful my sunglasses covered my tears.

The battle we fought could have ended so differently.

In continuing with the theme of gratitude and celebration, we hosted a big party—The Great Celebration! We had an open-house format, with people coming and going throughout the day and into the night. Julia, Micah, Jaron, and Michael took most of the cards received during our cancer battle and covered every inch of the staircase in the entryway, a visual reminder of the love and support gifted to our family from all over the world.

The Great Celebration *was* a great celebration. Darrin and Brent strung up lights in the backyard. We rented round tables and chairs, borrowed heat lamps and a bounce house. The food was wow! Leila did her decorating magic. Claire organized the day and figured things out on her Excel spreadsheet. God held back the rain. The best part? The people—people from near and far, who helped carry us through the year: friends from church and school, neighbors, ministry partners, Epic and PSW Cru staff, Darrin's Tuesday night men's Bible study group, my Wednesday Oasis friends, and my Wednesday night women's group.

After the sun went down, we gathered everyone around to share a few words of appreciation for them. Then Kelly's son, Matt, played his guitar and led us all in singing "Blessed Be Your Name" by Matt Redman. Darrin ended the night by praying a blessing over everyone who came.

"Father, thank you. Thank you for being here at the center of our celebration. Thank you for carrying us through this past year. Thank you for the friends who are here surrounding us tonight, and thank you for our friends and family who are here in spirit. Thank you for the blessing of community. Bless these men and women. Pour out your blessings upon them as they have poured out blessings upon our family. We are grateful. Thank you, Father. We are so thankful for you, Lord."

The folks in the Old Testament really knew how to have a good time because their celebrations would go on for days and days. Here in Mission Viejo, the celebration lasted ten hours—a little taste of heaven.

Remission

A few days after the big party, I had an appointment with my oncologist. I hadn't been back since chemo ended in June. Walking up the stairs to the office, I reminisced with Darrin about the first chemo appointment.

"Remember the first appointment? Remember how I had to stop here, halfway up the stairs, to rest? I was still so weak from surgery."

"Yeah. Seems like such a long time ago. So much has happened since the first time we set foot here."

It seemed a lifetime ago, and yet the feelings of returning to the office hit me hard. Tears filled my eyes as my hero-nurse, Karyn, came to my room to give me a hug. My doctor also greeted me with smiles and hugs.

My body reacted in funny ways to certain smells. I read what I experienced mimicked post-traumatic stress disorder. I could no longer use "Butterfly Flowers" shower gel. It reminded me of chemo. As did miso soup, Subway sandwiches, Yogurtland frozen yogurt, soda crackers, ginger ale, salsa with scrambled eggs, and my soft, green chemo blanket. The things that brought comfort during chemo now repelled me. Even certain songs on my iPod would take me right back to those awful, dark days.

Thank goodness sushi and chocolate escaped the banned items list.

During the appointment, the doctor told me I could now consider myself in remission. Apparently *cured* could not be used because they wouldn't know until I died if I was really cured from cancer. I would be scheduled for follow up appointments every four months for the next two years, and then every six months until I hit the five-year mark. Then I'd see her for an annual visit forever. My oncologist would become a friend for life.

After that appointment I started taking Tamoxifen, a drug that interfered with the activity of estrogen. My cancer, an estrogen receptor positive type, meant the cells had a protein to which estrogen would bind. The breast cancer cells needed estrogen to grow, so the drug worked against the effects of estrogen on those cells.

The doctor instructed me to take calcium and vitamin D every day for the rest of my life. They'd take blood panels every four months for a while to make sure everything stayed in range. I felt extra sensitive to every ache and pain. I wondered if cancer cells still lurked somewhere, a vulnerable place. I also found myself marveling, at the same time, how my body repaired itself and how far it had come (cue Destiny's Child "Survivor").

I left the office mostly encouraged and relieved.

Remission.

I liked the word.

Into Storage

I came home and took my Shasta sassy wig off the roll-of-paper-towel wig holder, which perched on the corner of my dresser for months and months. I collected a stack of cancer books, gathered various scarves and head coverings, notebooks full of notes and questions, medical logs, and other cancer-related paraphernalia. I gently placed the collection into an unmarked blue plastic tub. I put it in the already-full storage area next to my nook upstairs.

This experience was so vastly different than when I used to pack away my maternity clothes. I would anticipate who I could share the clothes with—which of my friends would be next to start on the journey that would end with a baby. I prayed this box would never need to be opened. Sadly, I knew the contents would be passed on eventually. But along with the contents would also come my heart—one transformed through the cancer journey and filled with compassion through firsthand knowledge.

I prayed I would be the kind of support and companion my friends and family had been to me to those who came after me. I prayed I would bring 2 Corinthians 1:3–4 to life for others, as it had been brought to life for me by all who battled with me: "Blessed be the God and Father of our Lord Jesus Christ, the Father of mercies and God of all comfort, who comforts us in all our affliction so that we will be able to comfort those who are in any affliction with the comfort with which we ourselves are comforted by God."

Solitaire

I had the whole house to myself on a rare Saturday morning. I slept in. By lunchtime I still wore my pajamas.

I continued to receive the post-active cancer treatment questions: "How are you doing? How are you feeling?" Kelly mentioned there would be a day when people asked "How's Viv?" and it would not be a question about my health.

We had not yet reached that day.

People asked because they cared, but the answer to their questions was so mixed. Every month I felt better and stronger, but on so many levels I hadn't fully recovered. Grateful to be in remission, yes, but I fluctuated between resisting the urge to jump back on the hamster wheel of activities and the frustration of not having the energy or desire to rebuild normal life. I found myself not taking my to-do list seriously, but also battling an inner compulsion to try and get to everything *now* because the future felt uncertain and I wanted to live every day to the hilt.

During this battle I coped by playing solitaire. Of course, even in checking out this way, my mind still raced. Life reflections according to solitaire went something like this:

Great starts don't necessarily mean great endings. I played countless games where I thought for sure I'd clear all the cards because the aces came out early and everything looked promising. But, in the end, the game ended with cards on the board and no more moves.

In the Christian life, strong starts don't necessarily translate to strong finishes. I had been around long enough to see spiritual wipe-outs. Strong starts, amazing zeal, great intentions gave way to either major fallout or quiet, passive falling away. I knew I was not immune to spiritual disqualification.

Seemingly hopeless cards can still clear. Sometimes the computer dealt what looked like "it's never going to happen" cards. Then, quite by surprise, they would clear. In life we don't see the end of the story. We don't know how things will end. There is hope even in the seemingly impossible. Which brought hope to the previous category of great starts and not-so-great endings.

Every game is different. Truth be told, I logged more solitaire games than I could count. I figured I would look back on the season of transition as the "Oh yeah, remember when I checked out by playing solitaire?" phase. Everyone handles difficult situations in different ways. I coped through solitaire. I played countless games and never played the same game twice.

So it is with life. My life didn't look like anyone else's. The challenges I faced and the frustrations, joys, pains, and circumstances were unique to the cards I was dealt. Now, I can only focus

CaringBridge

I went into my doctor's appointment feeling emotionally wobbly. Julia's classmate had a neighbor who died over Thanksgiving break from a four-year battle with ovarian cancer. Her daughter is Julia's age. I heard about the choices this woman made to help ease her passing. She insisted the family spend Thanksgiving away from their home and with close family friends. She died over the weekend, not on Thanksgiving Day. I imagine she thought about not wanting the family to have memories of her death in their home or on a major holiday.

I found her choices inspiring. A mother's love demonstrated to the end.

I still would appreciate your prayers this month as I go in for a couple more appointments and hit some of those dates that are "anniversaries"—but not really the celebrating kind.

on the cards in my life, and I am not responsible for the cards in anyone else's game. Darrin will play out his deck, as will each of the kids. It's tempting to want to play off someone else's deck. I'd become a master at being an armchair quarterback for other people's games.

But I needed, then and now, to focus on my game.

I continued my Bible reading plan. In the book of 2 Chronicles, I read snapshots of different kings, saw the choices they made and the outcomes of their choices. Each had a unique story with principles applicable to my life thousands of years later. In 2 Chronicles 20, enemy armies overwhelmed King Jehoshaphat. He prayed, "For we are powerless before this great multitude who are coming against us; *nor do we know what to do, but our eyes are on You*" (verse 12, emphasis mine). I kept chewing on those words as I tried to figure out how to live life after active treatment.

I did not know what to do, but my eyes stayed on Him.

11

the sensation
from swinging

"When you pass through the waters, I will be with you; and through the rivers, they will not overflow you. When you walk through the fire, you will not be scorched, nor will the flame burn you. For I am the LORD your God, the Holy One of Israel, your Savior."

Isaiah 43:2–3

As I mentioned, chemo turned my nails an ugly gray with deep ridges, so I kept them painted dark most of the year. My left big toe was especially affected. Not sure why. I watched as the unsightly part grew out over the months. Day by day, I could not track the growth, but over the course of weeks I noticed progress. Every milestone and event seemed to correlate with something to do with cancer. The school Christmas party for Julia came around again, and I signed up as the first parent volunteer.

The previous year, when we received the call from the doctor with the life-altering, derailing news from the biopsy report, we experienced a winter storm, so cold and dark. One year later, we planned to be with Darrin's family in Hawaii to celebrate Christmas—our first time in fourteen years to celebrate with our family in Hawaii. The kids couldn't wait to spend time with the cousins—*ten* cousins!

I chose to keep our Christmas decorating more low-key. Darrin wisely said, "Whatever is on your to-do list cut by two-thirds." Yup, my functioning capacity hovered at about one-third of my pre-cancer state. We got the tree up, decorated it, put some decorations in our front hall, and stopped. No outside lights and no decorations in every room of the house.

And it was okay.

NED

I went in for an ultrasound to thoroughly check my lymph nodes, scar tissue, and chest area to make sure the surgeries, chemo, and radiation obliterated any and all cancer cells. I set up the appointment without much thought and mentioned it in passing to Darrin. He asked me if I wanted him at the appointment.

"No, it's fine. I can just go." A little while later I came back and said, "On second thought, yes, I would like you there."

We sat in the same office where I'd had the diagnostic mammogram, ultrasound, and core biopsy back when the madness began. Over a year since I sat in those waiting room chairs. I found it disturbing, but familiar, to see the cancer magazines, informational flyers, and wig and hat pamphlets. The regular mammogram office, located on the floor below, meant every woman sitting in our waiting room faced a higher percentage of having her life radically altered. I felt grateful to not be alone like the first time—thankful Darrin had the wherewithal to know I still needed his support.

The appointment, though uneventful, still jarred me. Being escorted to the same room, lying on the same table, with the same machine, same smells, same sounds, rattled me. Knowing Darrin waited outside for me brought profound comfort. The ultrasound tech shared she, too, walked each day as a warrior in pink. She had undergone the same cancer treatments about a year ahead of me. I asked her questions about crazy curly chemo hair and various aches and pains feeling comforted by this fellow comrade in the battle. I finally asked her what I had wondered so long. "I'm curious. Since my cancer fell more on the slow-growing side, how come the other two mammograms I had at thirty-eight and forty didn't pick it up?"

She looked at me. "Funny you should ask. In the hallway just now, with your most recent mammogram, I asked one of the techs to find the cancer. The tech looked and looked, and then I told her, 'Look for a 4 cm by 6 cm mass.' She still couldn't find it until I pointed it out."

I guess denser tissue made mammograms less reliable or unreliable.

As she finished up the appointment, she handed me a yellow paper with my exam results. She had checked off the box *Normal: NED. NED* stands for *No Evidence of Disease.* I kept the yellow paper folded up in my notebook that I took to all my doctor's appointments. Each clear test result helped me exhale a little more. My confidence returned slowly.

But now I experienced more pronounced feelings of being lost, unsure, and confused.

Do you remember being little and swinging for hours on a swing or playing in the ocean all day or riding amusement park rides and then trying to fall asleep at night and having those sensations from the day still so close even though you are lying still?

Life felt like that.

New Take on Jeremiah 29:11

I hung a frame on the wall in my nook upstairs. My sister in law, Esther, gave it to me over Christmas. In it were three pictures of Hilo, Hawaii, and the verse: "'For I know the plans I have for you,' declares the LORD, 'plans to prosper you and not to harm you, plans to give you hope and a future'" (Jeremiah 29:11 NIV).

I kept staring at the picture and rereading the verse—turning what it meant over and over in my mind, like a slow rotisserie. I had committed the verse to memory years before, but now it seemed unfamiliar. I looked it up in different versions of the Bible. Some translated the Hebrew to say "plans for welfare," or "plans for good not evil," and some said "peace." I wrestled with my own thinking about my ideas of welfare and prospering and what it meant and how it looked played out in life. In my mind, living a long, pain-free life and seeing my children's children would be a wonderful plan for welfare, surely the best plan for my kids. But I wrestled with God anew over what the verse meant in the wake of the current earthquake in Haiti and, more close to home, with some of the heart-wrenching stories of people I knew who grieved unexpected death.

Prior to the past year I felt fairly confident I would grow old with Darrin. Now I no longer walked with the same assurance. I wasn't obsessed about death and dying, but unlike years past, those thoughts came on my radar in ways it hadn't before. I had to contemplate and embrace the truth that having cancer sometimes ended in death.

I needed to rethink and release my rendition of "plans to prosper." My plans may not line up with God's plans. Most people don't live out their "plan A." But somehow in God's economy, He wasted nothing. Even death.

As I brought my thoughts and concerns to God about a future both uncertain and unclear, He asked me, "Will you trust me? In your mind living a long life translates into the best way for the kids to love and trust me, but can you trust that I could use an unexpected death to bring them to a place of loving and trusting me? Can you trust that I see and I know and I have a bigger purpose and plan?"

I didn't see the end of the story. I had no idea how everything would play out. Instead of focusing on the plans, I leaned into the first three words of the verse: "For I know."

God knew.

That truth returned me to trusting God's character, His heart, His intentions, His goodness, His wisdom. It drove me to want to know Him and not just know about Him.

As I held on to Him instead of clinging to my plans, I experienced unexplainable peace.

Profound Relief

"Why doesn't anyone ever put anything away after they take things out of the cabinets or the fridge?" I slammed the cabinet doors shut and shoved dishes into the dishwasher—it's a wonder none of them broke. "What are all these piles? You guys need to take *everything* that belongs to you back into your room!"

I grabbed a sponge and wiped the counters with such force you could almost see smoke. I continued yelling into the air at no one in particular, hoping the kids took in my rants and felt remorse, guilt, and shame.

I thought my irritation and stress stemmed from not finding the counters under all the piles in the kitchen or because I couldn't find a chunk of time to work on the talks I would deliver in Dallas in a couple of weeks.

But then it hit me.

The MRI results distressed me.

I couldn't imagine reliving the past year.

The last time I had the MRI I *felt* totally fine, and ended up discovering I had a six-centimeter cancerous tumor. Not being able to gauge the test result by how I felt physically left me feeling uncertain and vulnerable.

I looked at the calendar and realized exactly a year ago I faced my first surgery.

I waited and waited for the phone call and checked and rechecked the phone messages to hear the results. Finally I called the office.

"I'm calling to get my test results."

The receptionist answered flatly, "What was the name again?"

I gave her my name and birth date and gripped the phone tighter as I waited to be transferred to the nurse.

Several minutes passed.

"Oh, hello, Mrs. Mabuni, sorry for the wait. I have your MRI results. Everything came back clear."

"Clear? So everything is okay?"

"Yes. Everything is okay." I loosened the grip on the phone and exhaled deeply as I hung up the phone.

Profound relief.

Tears of solace.

I think I would have sobbed if the kids hadn't been running around avoiding homework, annoying each other, and playing.

Muffs

Jesslyn did her magic, cutting away most of the "muffs," as she called them. Puffy, curly, clown, and earmuff looking hair above my ears. The initial hair growth first presented as baby soft, then looked chic and Halle Berry fashionable. Then came the embarrassing, unmanageable stage.

I needed serious help.

Jesslyn took out a bunch of the crazy curls collecting on the back of my head and cleaned things up. Much, much better. Leila loved me enough to tell me the truth: before the cut I looked like a Chinese grandma with my short, jet-black, tight-curl hair. Julia said I looked like a mad scientist with my crazy head of poofy hair. She laughed so hard she started to cry.

I loved to hear her laugh.

And I loved having hair.

Two Strands

If you walked into my closet and if you didn't fall over everything, you would notice my stuff outnumbered and outweighed Darrin's about four to one. He never, in almost twenty years of marriage, complained about how many pairs of black shoes I owned or about anything related to all my possessions in the closet. He is a good man. Truly. And not just because he doesn't give me a hard time about my belongings.

You would also notice on the wall inside the closet by the door, a misplaced plastic bathroom hand towel holder that had been added by the previous owners. It remained attached to the wall, oddly out of place the thirteen years we lived in the house. I hung a few belts from the holder, my Danskin triathlon medal, and the medal from the Huntington Beach Half Marathon. The newest addition? Two strands of hot pink Mardi Gras beads I received from the most recent Susan G. Komen Race for the Cure event. Each strand represented a year of survivorship.

I didn't know how to calculate survivorship. One woman I asked said she counted from the date of surgery when the surgeon removed the cancer. One doctor I asked said I could count from the date of diagnosis; another survivor said when I completed active treatment of surgery, chemo, and radiation. I decided I would wear a strand for every year I took part in the Race for the Cure event.

Unlike the previous year, this year the sun blazed on the day of the race. In fact we experienced unseasonably warm weather, so we decided to go on the earlier side of the day. Our family arrived in time to take part in the one-mile fun run. After the fun run, which we walked, was the tribute time for the survivors. I left Darrin and the kids under a shady tree. I worked my way through the crowd and up the steps to join the more than 1,500 survivors. We all wore the hot pink survivor T-shirts and carried in our hands pink roses. Each woman had varying numbers of those shiny, hot pink Mardi Gras necklaces draped around her neck.

Susan G. Komen's sister, Nancy Brinker, inspired me with all she had accomplished. Largely responsible for bringing breast cancer awareness into mainstream life, she helped change the world. The whole month of October no longer focuses on orange and black; it's become all about pink. NFL players and even Michael's football team had pink ribbon stickers on their helmets and pink shoelaces in support of breast cancer awareness. This kind of support didn't exist when thirty-year-old Susan G. Komen faced her breast cancer diagnosis and, shortly after, lost her battle with the disease in 1980.

Nancy shared her story as part of the tribute. The previous year I sat in the back of the survivor section to the right of the podium. This time I thought since I was in a different place, I would sit in a different place. I slipped into one of the empty chairs near the back of the survivor section on the left side and looked out over the sea of faces. I couldn't see the shady tree or Darrin and the kids from where I sat.

Suddenly I felt lost and alone. Then familiar small arms wrapped around my middle. I looked down, and Julia looked up and hugged me. I blinked back tears as she smiled and pointed to Darrin and the boys standing off to the side, right outside the survivor section. Both the boys had grown several inches over the course of the past year, now standing taller than Darrin. But my husband's broad shoulders remained unmatched. They reflected his strength and presence. Once again, Darrin had the wherewithal to know I needed the family close so I wouldn't feel alone.

The three of them smiled and waved—and I knew they were proud of me. Grateful tears filled up my sunglasses. We listened to a woman perform the Miley Cyrus song "The Climb" and watched as participants released doves into the bright blue sky. Julia and I joined the crowds as we cheered for another year and another strand.

nothing can hurry time

With the Lord one day is like a thousand years, and a thousand years like one day. The Lord is not slow about His promise, as some count slowness, but is patient toward you, not wishing for any to perish but for all to come to repentance.

2 Peter 3:8–9

It had been over a year since active treatment. Like a toddler learning to walk, I found myself initially falling down a lot and being emotionally unsteady as I returned to normal life. As the months continued, my confidence slowly began to return, but it didn't take much to knock me down. It didn't take much for me to find myself back on the floor in a heap.

In December, two years after I received my diagnosis, I felt as bewildered as I did when I first learned of my cancer. It seemed like everywhere I turned I read about women who died from breast cancer recurrence. I started reading a book my sister gave me written by her friend, not about breast cancer, yet the author shared two stories about her aunt who died from the disease.

I didn't look for these stories, but they kept popping up. Everywhere. As hard as I tried, I couldn't put the book down.

I felt a new level of vulnerability I had not experienced before. Cancer helped me learn to pay attention to how I really felt. I needed to understand how to bring my raw emotions to God. Most of my life I tried to numb my feelings with busyness or talking myself out of my feelings. But I learned valuable lessons as I identified and wrestled with my true, authentic emotions. I tried to be honest with myself, honest with God, and bring others in. I learned to be okay with a messy life and unpredictability.

CaringBridge

Hair silently marks the passing of time. The growth happens with slow, steady faithfulness, indiscernible from day to day. But over time, growth becomes evident.

During cancer treatment Julia and her friend, Anna, decided to donate their hair to Wigs for Kids. The cancer I battled left me bald and bewildered. But as we walked through surgeries, chemo, and radiation treatments, an unexpected outcome took place in my daughter's heart. Through the hard times, the tears, the questions with no answers, God started growing in Julia a heart to help and a desire to make a difference in the lives of others.

The daily struggle with food allergies has matured Julia; she has learned to talk

Mostly I felt vulnerable.

I did not like it.

Back There, Back Then

As the months sped by, I decided to buy a new Nike iPod chip for my running shoes. My old one ran out of juice as it sat unused in my closet. I loved using a running chip because it tracked the distance and speed of my runs. The information from the runs would upload to a Nike website. There I could see graphs of the total miles run, set up training programs or goals, and even use Google maps to figure out the distances of the courses I ran through the neighborhood. As part of the new theme with the new chip, I put together a new workout playlist on my iPod. My old playlists reminded me of life back then.

Back then, I ran every other day between three and four miles. Back then I conquered steep hills. Back then I weighed fifteen pounds less. The fifteen pounds I gained when I went through chemo (possibly because of the daily medication I took, a common side effect). The pounds could've also come from my metabolism slowing down from being middle-aged, or from post-treatment comfort eating.

Regardless, I felt discouraged.

Rather than being evenly distributed throughout my frame, the extra pounds decided to join my midsection. My heart longed for back there, back then.

I missed my life before cancer. I liked the new season of having all three kids in school all day, starting on my master's degree at Talbot, serving on the Epic National Executive Team, and having my own business card. I enjoyed working with the women's ministry at church. I experienced, for a brief time, life with some more tangible goals, direction, meaning, and purpose.

The further I moved away from back then, the better "back then" looked. But if I flipped through my journal from those days, I still had struggles, times of conflict with Darrin, confusion with how to navigate parenting, challenges with ministry and

with adults, parents, and waiters answering questions about what she can and cannot eat. When we went on a summer mission trip to Japan, one of the phrases she learned to say in Japanese was, "I am allergic to milk, peanuts, and eggs." At every birthday party she either abstains from the pizza and birthday cake or brings along her own little treat. A small handful of moms always go the extra mile to make sure the food they serve is "Julia friendly."

Feeling uncomfortable, misunderstood, or left out are familiar emotions for my daughter. And yet, these struggles have resulted in a depth of character not often seen in elementary school age kids.

So it shouldn't come as a surprise that when she learned her hair could help a kid battling cancer, she joyfully donated. I think her desire and understanding of how much this would help came on a deep level—from both knowing how it feels for a kid to struggle with feeling uncomfortable, misunderstood, and left out, and also from the first-hand experience of having a bald mommy. Following the initial cut, she allowed her thick, naturally highlighted, beautiful hair to grow.

Now, nearly fourteen inches of hair later, Julia sat extra still as the hairdresser cut her hair. My heart filled with gratitude (and my eyes were a bit misty) seeing her sitting in the chair, feet dangling. My own hair, now past shoulder length, covered the story of cancer that had marked our lives. Her long hair represented the long years of return to our new normal. Strangers came up to Julia when they learned what she was doing to let her know they were proud of her decision. In the end Julia, full of joy, collected her offering to help a kid going through a hard time similar to what we went through.

She wrote on the donation form: "My mom had cancer and lost all of her hair, and I realized I can

finances, decisions to make (including what to cook for dinner), deadlines, laundry.

Life.

I forgot that "back then" also had its share of struggles in the midst of the joys. I forgot it took time—a long, long time—and determination to get to a place where I could run hills.

I related to the Israelites in the Old Testament as they wandered in the wilderness after leaving Egypt. They longed for the "back then" of life in Egypt with garlic and leeks. They forgot the brutal treatment in Egypt and what slavery felt like. God provided, in the wilderness, water from rocks to drink, manna from heaven and quail to eat. Their sandals never wore out, not in the course of forty years. They witnessed God parting the Red Sea as they walked through to the other side on dry land. But despite the miracles, the longer the Israelites wandered in the desert and ate manna, the more their hearts longed for life back there, back then.

I used to find myself looking down on the Israelites at how quickly they forgot God and His miracles, or how they complained to Moses, or worshipped substitute gods. Now I see how very much I am prone to be like them.

Part of this post-treatment phase meant I had to embrace and accept that life would never be like back there, back then. Like the Israelites, I had witnessed God performing miracles and providing for us throughout the cancer journey. I learned lessons that could only be learned in the desert wilderness wanderings. God stood very near and was tender toward me throughout active treatment. I felt grateful for His mercy and grace, but I also found I had so many more unanswered questions.

Life didn't fit into neat categories anymore. I understood in new ways how and why people, like the Israelites, and like me, struggled to trust God.

help people by donating my hair."

I hate cancer. I hate how this disease takes lives. I hate the pain my family and friends walk through when they lose a loved one to cancer. I will never not hate cancer.

But somehow . . . battling cancer expanded our hearts and opened up our world to others. Julia is a shining example to me of beauty grown out of hardship.

I am proud of her and the growth I see in her life.

Eventually the Israelites arrived in the Promised Land, able to enjoy new food and drink, which I'm sure included garlic and leeks. But along with the benefits of being in a new land, they still needed to trust God—new battles to fight, choices to make, and new ways God revealed himself.

I still wandered around in the after-cancer wilderness. My head knew this phase wouldn't last forever, but it felt like forever. While in the desert I hoped to learn more about the state of my soul and what drove me to respond the way I did. I wanted to learn to trust God's timing of when to stay and when to move. Up ahead I'd face new areas to trust God, new battles to fight, and choices to make.

Instead of longing for "back then," I had choices and decisions each day in the here and now. So during Julia's soccer practice, I laced on those running shoes and, on mostly flat road, I ran longer than I walked.

I looked forward, not back.

Reentry Isn't Easy

I had follow-up appointments every three months with my oncologist, surgical oncologist, and radiation oncologist. Between those three doctors, it worked out to one appointment a month. Somehow all three landed in December.

I had blood work done the Friday after Thanksgiving in time for my Wednesday appointment. As I walked from the car to the office, a rush of memories flooded me. The waiting room, the smell of the air freshener in the bathroom, even the sound of my footsteps on the cement walkway all churned up dormant emotions. I now was in a different place, feeling physically strong. The scars from the surgeries and the port healed over as much as they would. I liked seeing the nurses and my doctor, but really, really, really, really, really strongly disliked being back in that office.

The doctor noted that my blood work was all in range, even my vitamin D levels. My body had started producing estrogen again, so I no longer felt pain when I got up from sitting on the floor. I could finally close my fists into a ball in the morning when I awoke.

I asked, with tears in my eyes, "When will I be able to move into the group of people who have battled breast cancer and now live life merrily on their way?"

She handed me a box of tissue and looked at me, compassion in her eyes. "What you are feeling is very normal. I have no reason to believe you won't be in that group. You have done everything possible to eliminate cancer. Your prognosis is excellent. It just takes time. Nothing can help but time."

I blew my nose and added, "I know. But I wish I could find a way to speed up time."

I understood. I knew all too well: Nothing can hurry time.

Right after that appointment, the news of Elizabeth Edwards's death from breast cancer recurrence filled the Internet, TV, and print media. I couldn't pull myself away from the articles. I calculated in my head—first diagnosed in 2004, and three years later it came back. Then I replayed what my oncologist said. News of women dying from cancer hit too close to home.

Leila wisely pointed out that the month would be rough because it was the anniversary of my diagnosis. When I thought about it, I realized that I had been extra edgy with the kids. I found myself tuning out and turning inside. I would sit, surrounded by piles of laundry, with the kids fighting and stare blankly at the wall. Darrin could tell when I started emotionally shutting down. At first I mostly felt dazed, but soon learned to pay attention to my heart. I could actually go a few days and not think about cancer, but it still stalked me. I even started thinking I was ready to jump back into normal life, but then an unexpected story or memory bowled me over and I felt flattened all over again.

When we worked closely with international mission projects, Darrin and I would brief our staff and students about reentry into American life after a short-term summer mission or year-long mission project. After living in a foreign land, people experienced typical responses to life back in their homeland. Often they'd experience a phase of frustration because people back home seemed shallow. Or they'd walk through a phase of loneliness because people around them didn't understand or care to know all about the country they came from. We helped people understand what reentry would feel and look like.

Now I needed to draw on the same principles. Our family had spent a year away in cancer land. This strange world had its own language and pace of life. Those who had not walked the soil of cancer land would not be able to fully relate to us. Just as those returning missionaries would not look at life the same way, we would never be the same.

But we knew One who never changed. One who is still the same after treatment as He was before. And that's what we held onto as we struggled to blend the two worlds we straddled.

Trying to Come Home

One night while on a Cru trip with Darrin and Julia in Colorado, my cell phone rang. Caller ID showed Jonathan.

"Mom, Max was hit by a car. I'm here with a neighbor who saw him bleeding on the street. She wants to know if we have a vet."

For the rest of the night we pieced together from three states away what happened. Weeks before I had asked dear friends if Max could stay with them while we attended our staff training. The boys would join us in Colorado, so Max would need a place to stay for a total of five days. The second day of his stay, when the husband came home from work and opened the garage door, Max darted out the door and took off.

We realized Max had tried to run home, even though the house was two miles away and we had only taken him to our friends' house by car. While trying to run across eight lanes of an extremely busy street, a driver hit him. Frightened and in shock, Max got up and ran all the way up a steep hill and into our neighborhood. A neighbor saw him bleeding on our front porch and rang our doorbell. Thankfully the boys were home packing their stuff before leaving for their trip. This wonderful neighbor stayed with the boys and took them to an animal hospital.

The mom in me wanted to hug my boys. I felt so helpless so far away. I learned from the intensive care vet that X-rays showed severe bruising in Max's lungs and a partial lung collapse from a tear. He had major laceration on his mouth; his paws bled; he was in shock, and his heart rate raced high.

The next day at the airport, we sat heartbroken in our silent world of pain, waiting for our boys to arrive. Finally, through the masses we saw familiar faces. The boys walked toward us, towering in the terminal. We'd only been apart from them four days, but they looked older. What they walked through seemed to have matured them somehow.

We swapped stories in the car. They shared what happened and what they knew. Hope filled our hearts as I shared the most recent phone call from the vet.

"Max is still on oxygen but he's stabilized. He made it through the night. The vet said if he could make it through the night he might make a full recovery. You know our Max, he is a fighter." The kids nodded.

We drove into Fort Collins and grabbed a bite to eat. The phone rang, so I took the call outside—another update from the vet. I kicked at the loose gravel in the parking lot as the vet said, "Mrs. Mabuni, I'm sorry. When we tried to help Max with his breathing, we found a huge pool of blood. Max had bled internally. The bruises on his heart were much worse than previously thought. His heart gave out."

"Wait. He's gone?"

"Yes. His heart stopped beating. I'm so sorry."

And just like that . . . Max died.

I hung up the phone. I stood alone in the parking lot, and inside, my family sat around the booth—somber but still hope-filled. At that moment, I alone knew the truth. I wanted to keep them from knowing.

I joined them at their table of half eaten burgers and French fries drenched in ketchup. I didn't know how to protect them and soften the impact of the news.

"That was the vet. Max's heart went out. He's gone."

Julia raised her voice in protest, "What?! Max is dead? He's really dead?"

I slipped into the booth, nodding my head. With my hands covering my face I tried unsuccessfully to muffle the wave of emotion welling up inside me.

Michael laid down in the booth with his arms covering his face as he cried aloud. Julia sat back and kept repeating "No, no, no" between sobs. Jonathan and Darrin, both pale faced, sat shocked and stunned.

When we left the restaurant, a light rain began to fall, as if heaven joined us in our grief.

That night I couldn't sleep. What if it had been me instead of Max? What if cancer took my life? What would it be like for Darrin to tell the kids? Was this how it would be for the family? Would they travel the same path of shock and despondency? Would the kids fall asleep crying in the dark, like they had tonight? Did my friends who lost loved ones to cancer walk through something similar to what we walked through today?

The kids and I had never walked through grief and loss. Darrin walked the painful road when his mother passed away during his junior year of high school. The following days and weeks Darrin gently guided our family. He laid out for us what to expect and allowed space for us to feel, to hurt, be angry, and to grieve.

Max came to us at a very tender time in our healing journey. We emerged from the battle with cancer so emotionally depleted. Darrin noticed we all drifted off doing our own thing, trying to cope. God brought Max into our family as an agent of healing. A reason for us to reconnect and bond. We lavished love and attention on him, and in return, he brought healing and reminders of God's perfect provision by his presence.

Now he was gone.

Remembering Max

The grief did not stop.
The grief came in waves.

Jonathan came into my room and shared, with tears falling, "I know at first I was the least willing to adopt Max, but I have absolutely no regrets. But, Mom, I have never walked through the emotions like the ones I'm feeling from losing Max."

I touched his arm, my tears joining his, "Oh, Buddy. It *is* so hard losing Max. We all knew someday he would die, but to have him die so young, so unexpectedly. I think it makes it even harder. Max really loved you, and I know you loved him. It's okay to feel, and hopefully it helps to share like we are."

We sat for a time together with no words, just connected in our shared grief.

Death grates against our concept of justice. And even though we know we will all die, when death arrives it still doesn't seem fair. Death exposes our vulnerability. It shows that we are not in control. Even the best medical care does not guarantee an extension of life. Battling cancer opened the real possibility of death to our family. Max's death created avenues for our family to talk about grief and death.

We hurt from death because we loved. We could try to shield our kids from the pain of death. Had we not allowed Max to enter our lives and hearts, we would have been spared the emotional devastation. But the joy he brought, the gift he was, made him worth the grief.

Max was just a dog, but he had become part of our family. He marked our lives, and we still shed tears for him. Our hearts will always, always miss him.

Dying to Know

"If you could know the exact day and time you would die, would you want to know? Why or why not? Turn to the person next to you and discuss."

So began Pastor Kevin's Sunday message. Completely caught off guard, my response to the question surprised me. Before cancer, I would have responded, "Yes, so I could best prepare my family and get things in order."

Everyone around me answered that way.

I didn't. Instead, I fought back tears for the rest of the service.

I didn't want to know.

I didn't want to know now because death had tainted the landscape of my life.

After church, back at home, I sat on the floor of our bedroom and shared my fears with Darrin and let the tears flow. These tears meant I grieved the loss of innocence—the only words I could use to describe the state of my heart. Before cancer, the thought of dying didn't occur to me—it was way down the line, off the radar, really. As a part of post-cancer life, I had to come to terms with the churned up emotions that came from treatment. I couldn't process them in that moment. But now, I couldn't keep from processing them. Or from realizing that after all I'd been through, I had a new perspective on death.

Like when I got engaged and then sat through a wedding ceremony.

Like discovering I was pregnant and noticing all the strollers and car seats.

Like watching a movie scene about someone having an allergic reaction and then having my own child with food allergies.

Like learning I was pregnant after having another miscarriage and struggling with allowing my heart to love a new baby I may never hold in my arms.

Weddings and car seats and food allergies and miscarriages had always been around, but now they felt personal.

Now I noticed every cancer billboard, radio commercial, TV ad, and every pink ribbon on a potato chip bag. When I received news of someone newly diagnosed, my heart would sink. Cancer was personal now. And death was no longer a far away, eventual kind of thing.

I didn't want to know.

But what I did want?

To live.

I found a difference between existence and life. I didn't want to spend whatever days God had for me merely existing. I wanted to live fully without fear.

I wanted to rest in the truth of Isaiah 46:9–10: "Remember the former things long past, for I am God, and there is no other; I am God, and there is no one like Me, declaring the end from the beginning, and from ancient times things which have not been done, saying, 'My purpose will be established, and I will accomplish all My good pleasure.'"

13

the beginning of the end and new beginnings

O LORD, You are my God; I will exalt You, I will give thanks to Your name; for You have worked wonders, plans formed long ago, with perfect faithfulness.

Isaiah 25:1

Leila would cheer me up during the dark days when I sat bald and discouraged with these words of hope, "When this madness ends, we must celebrate by visiting someplace amazing like Italy." Dreams of visiting Italy would get sprinkled into our conversations and during the hardest, bleakest times the prospect of walking about the streets of some new place helped me stay the course and finish treatment. Leila and I would pull up our frequent flier points online and check to see if the airline had any specials. When I hurt from pain and discomfort, Leila would cheer me up with visions of faraway places. We talked of visiting our Cru staff friends in Florence and Toulouse. In our search we discovered Rome hosted a marathon.

But then life took over and the weeks and months blurred. The everyday swallowed up the opportunity to visit the exotic locales.

Leila and I knew we would be in Orlando the first weekend of March for the Synergy conference, the one Debbie mentioned when she first shared about the *ezer* warrior. We attended the previous year and couldn't wait to return. Designed as a conference for women in leadership in churches, parachurch organizations, and businesses, the weekend would be filled with content geared to helping leaders lead and be world-changers for God's kingdom. We looked forward to being together again with other women of a similar heart and invited our friends from all over to join us. Our invitation yielded four: Lisa, Loi, Sonia, and Joanna agreed to join Leila and me making up what I affectionately termed, "the California Cohort."

Our conversation turned to visiting Italy in the Epcot center. Epcot would be the closest we'd get to Italy, but we still saw it as an adventure. We had booked our flights so that we would arrive a day before the conference started. We would take in Italy and France and the Middle East, and oh, pretty much the whole world, through Epcot.

The week before we left I saw the tickets for the Epcot center were $82. I couldn't see paying that much money since I had already spent so much for the flight, conference, and hotel. I hid my disappointment by talking the whole experience down in my e-mails with the cohort. "It's okay. It's too expensive. We don't have to go. We can just hang out by the pool at the hotel or go to the mall and just relax before the conference begins." I tried to let my disappointment dispel by looking forward to the other good things that would happen over the weekend. Again I found myself pushing down my hopes, desires, wants, dreams.

Then Joanna, from the triathlon, connected with a friend in California who had a daughter who worked at Disney in Florida. She had passes for three of us. Around two a.m. the night we arrived, we received a text from the daughter with news her boyfriend also worked at Disney. They could get all *six* of us in for *free* with Park Hopper tickets!

Yeeeesssssssssss!

The next morning we giggled and casually wandered our way through the Epcot center. No rushing about trying to squeeze everything in—we took our time. Lingered whenever we wanted. We hit Italy at lunchtime. Handsome Italian waiters with fun-to-pronounce names delivered twenty-dollar salads we had no hesitation ordering. We took pictures outside by the buildings made of stone, and we roamed around the fountain as Italian music filled the air. We stepped into the gift shop, and Lisa bought a book describing what different Italian hand motions meant. I picked up an Italy magnet to add to the collection of special remembrance magnets that filled our refrigerator door in the garage.

After our trip to Italy and France, we headed over to Japan to use the restroom. As we came out of the bathroom and our eyes adjusted to the bright sunlight, Lisa grabbed my arm. "Can you hear them?!"

We followed the sound. Our pace quickened. The banging grew louder. We began to run. My heart started pounding. Tears starting forming.

We arrived at the source of the sound. There, before us, drummed three *women* taiko drummers. All six of us knew the significance of the taiko drummers to me and how they had come to represent the marathon battle of cancer treatment. The woman drummers symbolized my journey embracing being created in the image of God as a woman, an Asian-American woman, an *ezer* warrior, a leader, a Christian. Those Japanese taiko drummers displayed both feminine beauty along with a "don't hold back, play with all your heart" kind of warrior strength.

And now, here at just the right time, at just the right place, with just the right people, the taiko drums played.

And we all stood there with no words and wept.

In that sacred moment, God spoke to my heart. "The end of the wilderness time has come," He said. In the Old Testament after Moses led the Israelites out of Egypt, the Israelites wandered around in the wilderness for forty years. God did not intend for the Israelites to live as nomad wanderers. He was clear from the beginning, promising

Abraham the land. The Israelites' wilderness wanderings had been a time of detour. Still, God redeemed the time. Their story did not end with walking in circles. While the drums played, I remembered that the cancer and its post-wandering time would not be my final destination.

So right there in the Epcot center in Japan, down the way from Italy, God sweetly, symbolically, showed me it was time to take up arms and reengage in life's battle.

The time of wandering had ended.

The cancer and post-cancer marathon had finished.

As the taiko drummers completed their performance, the six of us stood in awe and silence. We hugged each other as the significance of the moment sank in. I closed my eyes and lifted my face to feel the warmth of the sun. The theme verse God had shown me in the very first waiting room, the verse I clung to throughout and after treatment, came back to my mind like a favorite chorus from a song: "We went through fire and through water, yet You brought us out into a place of abundance" (Psalm 66:12).

Abundant Life

Battling cancer was a test, physically, mentally, and emotionally, of fire and water. God allows and uses fire and water in our lives to change and transform. Fire's heat purifies liquid gold and silver. It also reveals the quality or character of each person's work: "Each man's work will become evident; for the day will show it because it is to be revealed with fire, and the fire itself will test the quality of each man's work" (1 Corinthians 3:13). Water, though critical for the sustainment of life, also has the ability over time to cut through solid granite. God is faithful to bring us *through* fire and water, not give a life free from the challenges of the elements. He is also faithful to lead us to abundance.

In John 10:10, Jesus spoke these words of himself: "I came that they might have life, and might have it abundantly."

The original language for the New Testament is Greek. According to *The Discovery Bible*, the Greek word used for *life* in the verse was not *bios* (the period or duration of earthly life, or life extrinsic), but *zoe* (life in its principle, life intrinsic, including spiritual and eternal life). This abundant life Jesus offers is not one that is pain-free and smooth, but it is rich, rewarding, and often messy. Abundant life is not merely existing for seventy-plus years, but living life on another plane altogether. It's living in close connection with God, above circumstances and beyond what we experience with our five senses.

Abundance, in my mind, had always been a picture of bountiful grapes on a grapevine. One of my favorite Bible passages is John 15:4–5: "Abide in Me, and I in you. As the branch cannot bear fruit of itself unless it abides in the vine, so neither can you unless you abide in Me. I am the vine, you are the branches; he who abides in Me and I in him, he bears much fruit, for apart from Me you can do nothing."

Not long ago I learned that the best wine comes from grapes that experience an especially difficult season, be it drought or flooding. The drastic change in weather unleashes something in the grapes that produces an exceptional wine.

The parallels to life are too significant to overlook. We all know people who have walked through difficult seasons—with rain that doesn't seem to end, or dryness and heat that cracks the earth. Some become bitter and resentful and die on the inside.

But those who chose to sink their roots deep into God's Word and show up even after reaching the end of their physical limitations and emotional capacities are the ones who have learned intimacy with God. They walk through rather than run away—or numb away—from disappointment, grief, and despair. They abide or remain in the vine, even when the environment is extreme. And as a result, they display a beauty emanating from deep places.

These people become the exceptional wine, set apart in flavor and quality. They stand out. We admire them for strong character. That character comes through difficulty, discipline, and not giving up when circumstances threaten to take away life.

In wine country, some grapevines are over one hundred twenty-five years old. They no longer need to be watered. The root system runs twenty to thirty feet underground. The grapes produced from these vines are faithful, dependable, certain. And year after year, these grapes produce exceptional wine.

Fire and water trials are unavoidable. And as much as I want to protect my children from struggles, I know they will arrive at points in their lives when they will have to decide if they will move into the pain or try to numb it. Will the trials produce bitter hearts or exceptional character? From the time we returned home from the hospital with each of our kids, I have prayed that they would know and love God, and I have asked God to bless them with good friends, good mentors, and a strong sense of self. With a solid relationship with God, the help of friends, the input of mentors, and an understanding of who God has made them, I know they will be able to make it through whatever difficulties loom ahead. I have experienced this to be true in my own life. I want my kids to have what I consider to be more important than wealth, status, or education.

I want them to journey in community, known and loved deeply by God and by others—to live abundant lives.

Taiko Drummer Heroes

When it is time to go home to heaven, I picture Jesus greeting me at the finish line of my life playing taiko drums. Whether I am old, lying in my bed at home surrounded by loved ones, or I die much sooner, I sense I'll hear the faint sound of taiko drums beating steadily, calling this warrior in pink home. I picture hearing the sound grow louder and louder, finally freed from earthly suffering. I picture running toward Jesus, arms wide. I see His smile. I picture a sweet reunion with those I ache to see.

We are each given one life to live out the best we know how. The battle for life looks different for each of us, with different challenges, different lengths, different terrain. But each person begins his or her own race, and each person will one day end that race.

I see the heroes who have already arrived home. All of them playing those taiko drums. Nicole, Chris, Joel, Martha, Peter, Lorie, Christina, and the others I have known and loved and prayed for, all of whom lost their battle to cancer. I picture them greeting me.

And should I go home to heaven before you, I plan to welcome you into heaven, playing the taiko drums with reckless abandon.

appendix 1
sherpa: thoughts for caretakers

"Viv, you talk about how battling cancer was like a marathon run," Darrin said to me one day. "Well, while you were running the marathon, I also ran right along with you on the outside of the race tape—only I carried a huge backpack. No one cheered me on. No one held up signs."

Darrin drew this word picture for me as we sat in our marriage therapist's office. (I highly recommend couple's therapy during or after the cancer journey.) His attempts to explain what battling cancer from his perspective entailed finally made sense. Sadly this realization took a couple of years before I could hear his words without feeling responsible for the difficulties Darrin faced in my cancer diagnosis.

The battle against cancer, I think, often challenges the spouse or caretaker more. I asked Darrin what advice he would give to a spouse of someone recently diagnosed with cancer. Here are some of his thoughts:

- Move into it. The initial diagnosis can produce shell shock. Push through and move into what is before you.
- Take care of yourself too. It might feel selfish to feel needy during this time because you want to be all there for your spouse, but your needs are also important.
- Seek help for your spouse. You don't have to be the end all, be all. Having the Awesomes was so helpful because there

were times when I couldn't meet all of Viv's needs. That all the support, emotional and otherwise, didn't land on a single person was key.

- Try to have a few men around you to support you. Men sometimes don't like needing a support group, but having the support is key. My Tuesday night men's Bible study group strongly support me.

- Set up a support system for yourself early. It's too easy to isolate if a support system isn't in place, especially as the treatment keeps going. Having set times to connect with friends is helpful. Be proactive and set up those times in the beginning. The surprising thing is some people you think will be there for you won't be, but God will provide others you never expected to be there for you.

- Ask others to pursue you during this time, rather than having to keep initiating.

- Have the right people around. Jeff, Debbie's husband, shared, "Bro, there's no right way to 'do cancer.'" His were helpful words. Others, though well meaning, would give pat answers like, "just trust God." Not helpful words. There are moments of clarity and perspective when you have the wherewithal to pursue what you need, but sometimes you really need others to help you trust God.

- Sometimes it's helpful to connect with a spouse of someone who has battled cancer and can understand what you are going through.

I observed how emotionally draining it became for Darrin to be asked the same questions over and over again. Everywhere he went, everyone always asked how I was doing. Few took the time to really listen and find out how *Darrin* fared. Cards and flowers filled our fireplace mantle for me, signs of encouragement along the marathon path. Darrin kept pace right alongside me but in silence, unacknowledged.

His sponge for holding emotional pain filled up through our trial and resulted in a loss of capacity to absorb any more grief. In some ways both of our hearts had grown in compassion for those in chronic pain or struggling through medical trials, but we also found ourselves unable to respond with care and help to challenges we would have taken on before our cancer battle. At first this concerned me, but we knew that over time we would be able to move again toward emotionally draining events. We needed to give ourselves time and space to heal our hearts and spirits.

Two friends from church, Keith and Craig, took Darrin out for go-cart racing one night. I think it helped for him to play. After my active treatment finished, he took a well-deserved vacation to Nicaragua with some of the men in his Bible study.

It's vital for caregivers to remember that they, too, need care. And to find those who can support and care for them.

a thousand stitches: thoughts for parents with kids still at home

When Jonathan was eighteen months old, and Darrin and I lived in West Los Angeles, our Cru staff team at UCLA became our family because we didn't have immediate family who lived close by. Darrin's family lived in Hawaii. My parents lived in Hong Kong, and my sister resided in Colorado. Jonathan grew up calling our staff team and student leaders "Uncle and Auntie."

One morning while dancing around the living room waiting for his Uncles and Aunties to come over for staff meeting, Jonathan slipped and hit his head against the corner of the coffee table. As a first-time mom, I had the pediatrician's phone number on speed dial. After talking with the doctor, he determined we should have Jonathan go to the emergency room in case he needed stitches. My staff friend, Donna, joined me as we waited in the waiting room.

Finally, when it was Jonathan's turn, we learned he would need five stitches over his left eye. The doctor instructed me to hold Jonathan's upper body steady and have Donna hold his legs as they stuck a needle near his eye to numb the area. Twice.

To see my son scared and in pain gave me understanding of how moms find superhuman strength to lift a truck off their trapped child. This mama bear intensity also opened my eyes in a new way of understanding God's great love for us—how He finds no pleasure in our pain. I would have given anything to take Jonathan's place so he wouldn't have to have stitches. I would have taken a thousand stitches so he wouldn't have to have even one.

By far my greatest concern receiving a diagnosis for cancer was the welfare of my kids. Like the stitches, I would have done anything to spare them from having to walk through difficulty or pain. But rather than shielding them, Darrin and I determined together to let the kids know as much as we knew. We wanted them to hear directly from us, complete with the correct terms and definitions. We wanted them to know we trusted them with the truth.

Each family has a unique cancer journey. What worked for us may not work for others, but there are things, looking back, that we're glad we did. They are in no way a comprehensive list of "how to do cancer with kids." Some things were intentional; other things just happened in the course of what we faced.

We tried to keep life as normal as possible. Darrin and I wanted to keep the kids' schedule and activities as close as we could to life before cancer. This required an army of people movers. Three kids. Three sets of activities. Our friend, Lucy, an administrative wonder, set up a weekly drop-off/pick-up schedule. As a part of the temporary adjustment, the kids had to remember which car to look for during pick-up time.

Jonathan found high school to be a place where he wasn't surrounded by questions about my health. His church friends knew and were supportive, but it helped to have a place to go that remained cancer-free.

It was helpful to have close friends tracking with the kids emotionally. Leila would take time to check in with Julia to find out how she felt.

I chose to be bald at home to normalize life with chemo for the kids. I rarely wore my wig, as it was hot and uncomfortable. Going out,

I mostly wore scarves and hats. Since Darrin also shaved his head daily to stay bald with me, we looked like the Coneheads from vintage *Saturday Night Live* episodes. The kids got used to the bald look quickly. Years later I continued to hear how cancer impacted the kids. As we went along, I gained new insights to how our battle shaped their perspective on God, suffering, and relationships. In each kid's life, God used cancer to deepen his or her faith.

Jonathan and Julia decided to get baptized in our church the year following our cancer journey. Part of Jonathan's faith story was how the love and support from our church impacted him. By allowing others in to help us, we helped our kids see what true community looks like.

Julia wrote me a note in her first grade printing: "Dear Mom, I love you and the Lord will give you sranthe (*sic*) and will gide (*sic*) Daddy, Michael, Jonathan, and me!"

Michael shared how he wrestled with God, wondering how a good God could allow bad things. "You and Dad gave your whole lives to serving God as missionaries, and then you got cancer. It just didn't make sense." Yet through our cancer battle and his own struggles with illness and broken bones, he emerged a more grounded follower of Christ. "I learned how I had put my confidence in being strong and invincible, but God used your cancer and my own physical setbacks to show me how only He is truly strong and invincible."

During treatment, the kids still fought with each other and had bad attitudes at times, so things continued on quite normally in the Mabuni household.

My worries about the kids continue (I am learning this will be a lifelong tension as a parent). I remember waking up at 4:30 in the morning, after my second surgery, to take more pain medication. Sitting in the quiet of the house with the darkness all around, I began to pour out to God my concerns for the kids. That morning I read in the

Bible Psalm 115:12–15: "The LORD has been mindful of us; He will bless us; … He will bless those who fear the LORD, the small together with the great. May the LORD give you increase, you and your children. May you be blessed of the LORD, maker of heaven and earth."

We experienced that God had, indeed, been mindful of us and blessed us. He blessed our children through the help of so many.

letter to a newly diagnosed cancer patient

Recently people reeling from the "You have cancer" diagnosis have contacted me. If I could, I would sit down with them "in human" by the fireplace at my Starbucks and listen to their stories. I wouldn't give them advice unless they asked me. If they asked me, I would share with them a few thoughts for those newly diagnosed with cancer from the perspective of a cancer survivor.

Dear Bewildered Friend,

I am so sorry you are replaying in your mind the cancer phone call from your doctor. Everyone around you is living life just as always, and here you sit with news so heavy, so derailing.

If you are like me, nights are the hardest. After the house quiets down, you lay there alone with your thoughts and fears. And each morning you wake, wondering if all of this is a bad dream. Once you regain your bearings, you're faced with the challenge of getting out of bed to face another day. Physically everything looks the same; but now with this devastating diagnosis, nothing is the same.

If you've started sharing the news, I imagine your phone is ringing and your e-mail inbox is filling with well-meaning friends and family offering advice on diets, doctors, and blog links and books. If you are like me, you will probably try to read everything, and then hit a wall of information overload.

You've been abruptly thrust into a new world filled with unfamiliar terms and options, appointments, decisions, all with varying outcomes. It's hard to sort through all the information to know which steps to take.

These are just a few nuggets of advice from me looking back on my cancer battle. Feel free to apply what you like or disregard them altogether.

- There is no right way to do cancer. Everyone's cancer journey is different. Yours won't look like anyone else's. So give yourself freedom to be on your own path.
- Let others in. Chances are those who love you feel incredibly helpless and scared and want to help you in any way they can. Giving them the opportunity to bring a meal, drive you to a chemo appointment, clean your bathroom, or pick up your kids is a way for them to lessen the load for you, and it can be a blessing for them. Let others help so you can have space to heal and physically and emotionally tackle each portion of active treatment. You'll probably be surprised, though. Some people you thought would be there for you may disappear, and people you didn't expect may come along to help.
- Find an information hub person. If you're married, your spouse won't be able to go anywhere for the next two years without being asked how you are doing. Family and friends will want updates. We stopped answering our home phone. Rather than saying the same thing over and over, consider using an online site like CaringBridge for updates

and prayer requests. If you enjoy writing, writing updates on the blog may be a good way to process your journey. If you don't, ask someone to write updates for you.

- Try to be generous in the grace department. Grace is unmerited, undeserved favor. Give yourself grace. You've never battled cancer before. You are entering uncharted waters with how you will respond physically, emotionally, spiritually, and relationally. Don't be hard on yourself. Give those around you grace. They want to help, even though their unsolicited advice, like the latest cancer-killing vegetable discovered in the rain forest, may not be helpful. Your cancer diagnosis may trigger unresolved grief in those around you, so sometimes their response may not be what you need or want.

- Lean into God. Wherever you are in your spiritual journey, my encouragement is to move toward God. He can take your anger, your confusion, your sadness, your fear. Be honest with Him. He wants your whole heart. Let Him help you, comfort you, provide for you. And let others pray for you. God is able to bring good out of something as awful as cancer.

I hate cancer. I hate thinking about another person having to battle cancer. I hate that you will walk the painful treatment road. As much as I hate cancer, I want you to know from my experience that God used cancer to expand my heart. I have met some of the most remarkable people on this journey. I have been blessed in thousands of ways by the thoughtfulness and generosity of so many. I am not the same woman today because of cancer.

Cancer has marked my life, but it does not define my life.

I am praying for God's blessing on your life in unexpected ways.

> Love from a fellow
> warrior in pink,
> Viv

acknowledgments

I had no idea.

It took cancer to pull out the writer in me. During the early years of parenting, my ears fell deaf to Darrin's steady encouragement to put words to page. I felt insecure and untrained. Darrin saw the writer in me before anyone else. I had no writing background, no prior writing experience, so I kept brushing off the urging of friends to turn my website used during cancer treatment into an actual book. And yet against all odds the book is here. Thank you to those friends who kept encouraging me to write: Steph, Di, JL, Audrey, Joann, Marjilou, Toni, Flora, Shane, Nicole, Julie, Carrie, Sherry, Lena, Warren, Alane, Margaret, Heidi, Faye, Irma, Margee, Tracie, Nancy, Melissa, and Chrissy.

God's guidance and provision throughout the publishing process has been undeniable. Part of this provision includes the army of friends and family who prayed, cheered and spoke words of belief. To mention each and every person would require adding another 200 pages to the book.

I would, however, like to highlight and thank some influential leaders who came alongside and opened doors of possibility and opportunity.

I am grateful for Judy Douglass. Serving under her godly leadership on staff with Cru is a privilege. Judy's passion to live out her life mission as an encourager, *"urging everyone I encounter to know God and to entrust their lives to Him for all He wants them to be and all He has prepared for them to do"* set the writing ball in motion. Thank you for reading my journal entries, praying me through cancer treatment, inviting me to share a guest post on the Cru women's website, and for your steadfast support.

Thank you, Elisa Morgan. You offered godly counsel, encouraging me to "jiggle the doorknobs" and you opened the door for my first article to be published in *Fulfill*. Helen Lee and Tracey Bianchi, meeting you at the Synergy Women's Conference came after the "taiko drums moment." Your belief in the "someday book" and sharing about the importance of writing in community proved foundational. My appreciation runs deep for you, Helen. You patiently mentored me and generously provided sound input and advice throughout the proposal process. I am grateful to Carolyn Custis James who wrote words of hope and strength through her teaching about the *ezer* warrior.

So grateful for Aaron Schweizer who spent untold hours setting up my first website. Thank you, Mark Chang, for taking the photos used on my website, speaking profile, and back of this book. Thank you Cal Bible study (May, Becks, Bessie, Lisa, Kristen, Sandra) for gifting an extra night at the Fairmont so I could write. And thank you to the sisterhood of the Redbud Writers Guild, especially Karen Yates and Ann Suk Wang, who have celebrated each hurdle cleared and offered advice, support and timely encouragement.

What a blessing to work with Discovery House Publishers. A special thank you to Miranda Gardner, the managing editor, who discovered me through author Julie Ackerman Link. Miranda's Facebook message requesting my book proposal began a string of e-mails from her over the course of a year. Each had me alternating between screaming into my pillow and running through the house waving my arms wildly with excitement and astonishment. I've so enjoyed working with Miranda and with Anne Bauman, publicist at Discovery House.

Thank you to Oceanside Christian Fellowship and Crossroads Community Church for the scholarship, which opened the doors to attend the Mount Hermon Writer's Conference. I met incredible folks in the publishing industry including my literary agent, Karen Ball, and Steve Laube, the president of the agency who now represents me. My gratitude abounds for Karen's friendship and vast experience in the publishing world. Thank you for speaking those magic words with tears in your eyes, "Wow. You can write." And thank you for the priority you place on family and marriage before writing. I look forward to many more years and God willing, many more books, and walking the writing road together.

Thank you to Mary DeMuth for her brilliant editing skills. Mary's warmth, encouragement, attention to detail, patience with this inexperienced author, and helpful suggestions helped draw out more layers and texture for the story. Mary's example and generous, shepherding heart inspires me. I hope to be like you one day.

Thank you to Valerie Hon for opening her beautiful guesthouse to me during the grueling long days of editing. Valerie shared perspective, wisdom and encouragement at just the right times, and provided a steady flow of delicious vanilla lattes, fruit, chocolate and sushi.

The subtitle of the book, *A Story of Cancer, Community, and the God Who Comforts*, captures what I believe are the most important ingredients in any type of trial. I'm grateful for the community who loved my family and me so well. Deepest heartfelt thanks to our Crossroads Community Church family. Your generosity and help is unmatched. Thank you to my incredible medical team of nurses and doctors. Thank you to our ministry partners, staff friends and our family and friends who gave generously to help with our medical expenses. Thank you to each person who took time to pray for us.

My appreciation overflows for each of the men who attend the Tuesday night Barn Bible Study. Thank you, Gentlemen, for being a strong support to Darrin. He is blessed, and in turn our family is blessed, to have you as brothers in the faith. Special thank you to the

Wednesday Oasis Bible study women: Missy, Elaine, Annie, Mellanie, and Paula and my Wednesday night "balcony friends." You have modeled courage, honesty and integration. Thank you to our Epic Movement staff and Cru staff friends. What joy to labor with you for our King and for His kingdom.

Thank you to our Ohana in Hawaii: Dad, Dylan and Lisa, Marshall and Esther, Jon and Debbie and amazing nieces and nephews. Your prayers and strong support were felt coming halfway across the Pacific. And thank you to my Dad and Mom and sister, Claire. Thank you for your firm belief the book would happen and for your generosity and helping us in so many tangible ways.

The Awesomes and spouses and kids: Leila and Brent, Kelly and Dave, and Debbie and Jeff. Words cannot adequately describe my gratitude. You love so well and you demonstrate the steadfast love of God. Just thank you. A million times over.

Jonathan, Michael, and Julia, what an honor to be Mom to the three of you. I am so proud of who you are and who you are becoming. Watching you discover and live out who God has made you is pure joy. Every milestone you reach I celebrate and treasure. Thank you for being wonderful in every way.

Darrin, you are indeed the strongest man I know. You are also wise, authentic, passionate, generous, tenderhearted, creative, and tenacious. Thank you for living out our marriage vows and not giving up. Thank you for being an advocate, for welcoming my voice and fighting for our family. Through the ups and downs, highs and lows, good times and hard times, I'm grateful to journey with you.

Finally, thank you, Jesus. I am grateful for the gift of life, both eternal and for each day you give here on earth. You are mysterious in all your ways and a God of redemption, comfort and kindness. Hope in you does not disappoint. May the words written in this book honor you and lift you high.

> *For from Him and through Him and to Him are all things.*
> *To Him be the glory forever. Amen.*
> Romans 11:36

note to the reader

The publisher invites you to share your response to the message of this book by writing Discovery House Publishers, P.O. Box 3566, Grand Rapids, MI 49501, U.S.A. For information about other Discovery House books, music, or DVDs, contact us at the same address or call 1-800-653-8333. Find us on the Internet at dhp.org or send e-mail to books@dhp.org.

about the author

Vivian Mabuni joined the staff of Cru (Campus Crusade for Christ) twenty-five years ago and has served on the UC Berkeley and UCLA campuses and on the Epic National Executive Team (Epic is the Asian-American ministry of Cru). Vivian enjoys teaching and training college students at conferences and retreats and speaking at women's events. She has been married twenty-two years to her husband, Darrin, and is mom to three wonderful kids, Jonathan (20), Michael (17), and Julia (12). They live in Mission Viejo, California, along with their German shepherd, Koa.

You can connect with Vivian by:

- Becoming a fan on Facebook: facebook.com/VivianMabuniWriter
- Following on Twitter: @vivmabuni
- Following on Instagram: @vivmabuni
- Following on Pinterest: pinterest.com/vivmabuni
- Visiting her website: www.vivianmabuni.com

If you found this book to be helpful, will you consider sharing the message with others?

- Write a review on Amazon.com, bn.com, or Goodreads.
- Mention this book in a Twitter update, Pinterest pin, Facebook post, or blog post.
- Instagram a picture of you reading the book (tag me: @vivmabuni).
- Pick up a copy for someone you know who is battling cancer or has someone close battling this unwelcome disease.
- Visit facebook.com/VivianMabuniWriter, "LIKE" the page, and post a comment as to what you found most helpful.
- Tweet "I recommend reading #WarriorInPink by @vivmabuni// @DiscoveryHouse."

You can read more from Vivian at www.vivianmabuni.com.